123

R £3

CW00495006

Dancing with Mortality: Reflections of a Lapsed Atheist

Bert Clough

Copyright 2020 © by Bert Clough

All rights reserved. No part of this publication may be reproduced, distributed or transmitted in any form or by any means, including photocopying, recording, or other electronic or mechanical methods, without the prior written permission of the publisher, except in the case of brief quotations embodied in critical reviews and certain other non-commercial uses permitted by copyright law.

Dancing with Mortality: Reflections of a Lapsed Atheist
Bert Clough-1st ed.

ISBN 978-1-8381695-0-3

Cover illustration by Samuel Batley
Book design by Garth Stewart

Contents

Dedication

This book is dedicated to the Revd Dr David Usher, whose authentic and thoughtful sermons opened up so many spiritual windows for me.

Acknowledgement

I am deeply indebted to Catherine Robinson of Manchester College Oxford Chapel Society for her professional skill in copy-editing the text.

Preface

Almost twenty years ago, a middle-aged, lapsed atheist took his first step across the threshold of a Unitarian chapel. It was the eighteenth-century Meadrow chapel in Godalming, and I had no idea of what I was walking into. For most of my adult life I had been an unthinking atheist. But I felt I needed another dimension to my life, which at that time was trapped in some existentialist torpor. I didn't need a creed, but perhaps a religious framework for my evolving humanism, which underpinned my long-held social and political progressive views.

I was therefore fortunate that my first service was led by the chapel's then minister, David Usher. His message was that religion had to be authentic. It should be not be based on what we state we believe in by mouthing outworn creeds, but on how we behave, and the "sanctity of our soul". Unitarianism was not about the "right belief". Authentic faith meant that you are encouraged to take your own unique experience in life and to craft it into your own understanding which makes sense to you as an individual and sustains you in times of crisis. There were many ways you can do this, and the wondrousness of Unitarianism is that they can be expressed and practised in one religious community where there is no commonality of belief. More important is the commonality of purpose which helps us through the twists and turns of our disparate life journeys.

This profound message made great sense to me and was to open many windows. It even led to the honour of conducting occasional services at that beautiful, simple, chapel which for many years was my spiritual sanctuary. So, this book is not written by a minister or a theologian but by an amateur, a Unitarian lay preacher. It is written by a generalist for the general reader. It therefore does not profess to offer any unique insights into Unitarianism. The chapters are derived from sermons that I have preached over the years at Meadrow Chapel and Manchester College Chapel, Oxford. They have been expanded to develop the themes and provide more space for reflection than a 20-minute sermon allows.

Hopefully, these sermons were not regarded by the Godalming and Oxford congregations as preachy. They were meant to be eclectic in nature and they are, in many ways, contradictory. They are not about my rather undeveloped beliefs. I try to understand challenging issues through the lenses of spiritual leaders. That is why some chapters centre on the beliefs and authentic lives of spiritual teachers such as Dietrich Bonhoeffer, the Buddha, Norbert Capek, Jesus Christ, Dorothy Day, Mahatma Gandhi, Gustavo Gutiérrez, Albert Schweitzer, Wainstill and Martha Sharp, and Simone Weil. Many of them were not Unitarians, but they shared our liberal values. It was humbling to research their authentic lives, plumb their spiritual depths, and marvel at their huge personal sacrifices. Other sermons centred on more general themes such as whether we need God; the efficacy of prayer; ethics and religion; war and peace; anti-Semitism; and the relationship between politics and religion. I certainly enjoyed preparing the sermons and even found the process developmental.

A Principal of Mansfield College, Oxford often told his students that their sermons "would not save the soul of a tomtit". It is fortuitous that the Revd Dr Selbie never had to listen to any of mine. My aim, however, was not to save souls. If congregants left the services with more questions unanswered than when they arrived, then I felt that I had succeeded in my mission.

Bert Clough
September 2020

What kind of religion is this Unitarianism? It is humanity lightened by divinity. It is humanism and theism combined. It is not the kind of humanism without God and without a soul, but the humanism of those great individuals who from time to time called our nation to a new life... What else is it but to begin with humankind when seeking God?
(Revd Dr Norbert Capek, 1870-1942, Unitarian martyr).

1 Beyond Heaven and Hell

> *The task of religion is not to turn us into proper believers; it is to deepen the personal within us, to embrace the power of life, to expand our consciousness, in order that we might see things that eyes do not normally see.*
>
> (John Shelby Spong; b. 1931, retired Episcopalian bishop)

When the comic actor and lifelong atheist W. C. Fields was on his deathbed, a visitor found him reading the Bible. Asked what he was doing, he replied, "Looking for loopholes, my friend. Just looking for loopholes." Heaven is traditionally thought of as the place where God lives, which he shares with the angels, saints, and chosen dead. Hell, on the other hand, is somewhere that is completely separated from God and is the home of the Devil. The Book of Revelation sets out what is in store for us:

> *To the thirsty I will give water without cost from the spring of the water of life. Those who are victorious will inherit all this, and I will be their God and they will be my children. But the cowardly, the unbelieving, the vile, the murderers, the sexually immoral, those who practise magic arts, the idolaters and all liars – they will be consigned to the fiery lake of burning sulphur.*

The list of the damned is so long that before the stragglers got to the lake the fire would have long gone out.

As a boy, I was taken to see a thirteenth-century mural in the church of St. Peter and St. Paul in Chaldon, Surrey: "The Ladder of the Salvation of the Human Soul, the Road to Heaven". It is divided into two halves; the lower half graphically depicts the torments and punishments of the wicked, while the upper half is devoted to the salvation of the souls. A ladder leads from the lower to the upper world. A winged St. Michael is weighing the souls, and the claw-footed Devil is trying to bear down the scale with their bad deeds. A pathetic figure clings to the ladder to try to climb to the celestial level, but the Devil is about to pitchfork him into the fiery cauldron. It was the stuff of nightmares; such images were reality to most supplicants in the Dark Ages, before the Enlightenment shone a torch on such superstition. But "fire and brimstone" preaching is still found even today in some fundamentalist religious sects.

I am more comforted by a Kaddish prayer that I once heard at a Jewish funeral:

> *Oh God, full of compassion, who dwells on high, grant true rest upon the wings of the Divine Presence, in the exalted spheres of the holy and pure ... Therefore, may the All-Merciful One shelter him with the cover of His wings forever, and bind his soul in the bond of life. The Lord is his heritage,*

The birth of religion goes hand in hand with the evolution of human consciousness. The former Episcopal Bishop of Newark, John Shelby Spong, offers us an interesting narrative on this development. Embryonic forms of consciousness in animal life began as an adaptive, survival-related mechanism. They responded to the threat of the moment. They could not anticipate tomorrow's traumas. They had no need of religion as a source of emotional security. Then, out of the line of primates, a species emerged with a larger brain. They were human-like, but not yet fully human. That was the critical moment when consciousness expanded into "self–consciousness". It was crossing the Rubicon that separates conscious life from self-conscious life. No-one knows when this transition took place. Some scientists think that it was two hundred thousand years ago. Others date it as recently as fifty thousand years ago. These self-conscious creatures began to experience themselves as separate from the world of nature, of which until that moment they had simply been a constituent part.

This consciousness is seen in the cave murals in Lascaux, France, painted in around 17,000 BCE. The paintings in this "pre-historic Sistine Chapel" depict as many as 6,000 figures such as deer, bulls, horses, and humans. One of the oldest artefacts in the British Museum, *Swimming Reindeer*, was intricately carved out of the tip of a mammoth tusk in the Ice Age by Neolithic man. This early art depicts the spark of human imagination and heightened consciousness that separates human beings from other sentient animals.

Humans now perceived themselves as being in a world that dwarfed them, encouraging feelings of weakness and even helplessness. They wanted to shelter inside something bigger than they felt themselves; a comfort blanket. They began asking uncomfortable questions of purpose, meaning, and destiny. Unlike other animals, self-conscious people recognised that life was transitory. They had to embrace mortality, knowing that in the end nature devours all its children. Humans are the only animals for whom their own existence is a problem that they have to solve. The dinosaurs did not tremble at the moment before their extinction. So how do we overcome this existential angst? Spong puts it like this:

> *The only way that I will know what it means to live is to discover what it means to die, and in a contrary manner, the only way I will know what it means to die is to discover what it means to live.*

So, we need to dance, not wrestle, with mortality. A supernatural, theistic God was thus created to be a human coping device, and the human system named religion empowered the ruling figures of both king and priest. It is based on a supernatural yet essentially materialistic view of an afterlife.

I encountered the absurdity of such a materialistic conceit when I once visited the beautiful cathedral in Pisa. I was told that when it was being built in the twelfth century the spoil was discarded on an adjoining piece of land. This began to be used for burying the construction workers who died working on the site. The remains of these unfortunates began to disintegrate much more rapidly than in any other graveyards. This was because of the presence of a certain mineral in the spoil. Now at that time the Catholic Church believed that you could not enter heaven until your bones disintegrated. So, all the nobility of Tuscany who wanted a quick ticket to heaven bought a plot, and the Cathedral made a fortune in selling them at astronomical prices. A win–win situation, except, of course, for logical reasoning.

One of the early signs of the demise of traditional ideas concerning the afterlife is seen in the rise in the Western world of what might be called "liberal politics". If God was believed to provide redress in another realm, the obvious inequities in life – when the good die young and the charlatan lives to a ripe old age – then there was no need to redress this unfairness in this life.

> *Righteous art thou, O Lord, when I plead with thee: yet let me talk with thee of thy judgements: Wherefore doth the way of the wicked prosper? Wherefore are all those who are happy that deal very treacherously?*
> Jeremiah 12.1

It was when this injustice was challenged that liberal democracy, based on an enlightened humanism, emerged. Although the material concepts of heaven and hell have diminished in recent times– with the exception of fundamentalist thinking – there seems to be a kind of void. The liturgy and the icons of heaven and hell are stubbornly present in established churches, with its priests struggling to keep up with rapidly evolving scientific knowledge and social progress. Many are spending their lives dragging the decaying carcass of outworn beliefs.

The present challenge for radical theologians is to push against the supernatural concept of the world. The turn from the deity 'above' to the deity 'within' is an enormous shift, and many of us struggle to make this leap. We have been helped by non-creedal churches, such as Unitarianism, which have stopped talking about heaven and hell as future places but as ways of understanding our everyday lives here and now. Heaven can be thought of as a state we are in when we are at peace, and hell as the state we are in when we are in torment. The great strength of Unitarianism is that it imposes no creeds but provides the space to develop our own authenticity on our disparate spiritual journeys.

Can life after death, however, be entirely freed from the outdated ideas of our past? To do this, the religious barnacles clamped to the old concepts of a supernatural God need to be scraped away. We need to douse the flames of hell and unhinge the pearly gates of heaven. As Spong says:

> *If you and I live our lives motivated by our desire to enter paradise or to avoid punishment, then we have not escaped the self-centredness of life that is so natural to survival-oriented, self-conscious creatures.*

The way forward according to Spong is to move from our self-conscious life to a heightened consciousness. It is not about abandoning religion but about transcending the politics of the old religion – which separates true believer from heretic; the saved from the unsaved. Spong argues that Jesus Christ stepped from self- consciousness into this universal consciousness that brings us into a profound oneness with all there is. He had become one with God. Stepping into this consciousness is perhaps entering a form of mysticism:

> *The task of religion is to seek humanity that is not governed by the need for security, but is expressed in the ability to give ourselves away. It is to live not frightened by death but rather called by the reality of death to go into our humanity so deeply and so passionately that even death is transcended.*

Unlike Spong, I come from a humanistic background, and as a result I have had to live without a security blanket. During a particular period of my life I did experience an existentialist angst about my own mortality and was enveloped in a grey cloud of nothingness. That is why I stepped over the threshold of a Unitarian chapel. I have not yet attained this heightened, universal consciousness, but I am slowly beginning to understand that death is not the end. Indeed, the knowledge of certain death gives vibrancy to our living. There is an invisible, yet strong, thread linking life with death. Maybe we fear death because we cannot imagine the world without our presence; but is that not also true of a world that we had not yet been born into? The Greek philosopher, Epicurus, tells us that death should not concern us, because so long as we exist, death is not here – and when it does come, we no longer exist. Kahlil Gibran in *The Prophet* is even positive about death:

> *If you would indeed behold the spirit of death, open your heart wide into the body of life. For life and death are one, even as the river and sea are one. ... For what is it to die but to stand naked in the wind and to melt into the sun? And what is it to cease breathing, but to free the breath from its restless tides, that it may rise and expand and seek God unencumbered?*

On contemplating his imminent demise, the Unitarian Universalist minister, Forrest Church, felt great comfort:

> *Being agnostic about the afterlife, I look for salvation here – not to be saved from life, but to be saved by life, in life, for life .... My life feels like it is concluding; this period has the feeling of a coda to it. I feel I've done what I needed to do. I look back without regrets and I look forward without fear. I've never been more in the present.*

As I have grown old, I have seen many loved ones die and perhaps I have spent too much of my time mourning their departure. But the deceased that we have been close to are, in reality, still with us. Indeed, they remain part of us. Perhaps all that we need to do is to filter out any negative feelings for the deceased, and indeed the living, that might torment us; that trap us in a personal hell. Instead, we need to celebrate and magnify their goodness so that it becomes an integral part of ourselves. We, in turn, can pass on this loving kindness to others who then can pass it on to others, ad infinitum: a chain reaction of compassion. We then might have left a tiny bit of heaven on earth and added a drop of goodness to the vast ocean of eternal love.

Sources cited in this chapter

Book of Revelation 21:5–8.

Forrest Church: *Love and Death. My Journey through the Valley of the Shadow.* Houghton Mifflin Harcourt, 2008

Kahlil Gibran: *The Prophet.* William Heinemann Ltd, 1980.

John Shelby Spong: *Eternal Life: A New Vision.* HarperOne, 2010.

2 Christ without God?

God is that great absence
In our lives, the empty silence within
(R. S. Thomas)

The late Margaret Hamer, a member of the Bury St. Edmunds Unitarian congregation, described herself as a religious humanist. She was relieved to encounter God as neither He nor She, but more commonly as something unknowable, or a profound silence. In her words:

> *To claim simultaneously that a supreme being exists beyond both our language and our comprehension, and yet to persist in attempting to delimit it within terms such as father/mother, creator/goddess, seems contradictory to me.*

There are probably as many Unitarian views on God as there are Unitarians. They might describe God as a universal father or mother; or as a unifying and life-giving spirit; or as the source of all being within which the creative process is unfolding. Some might even be theological theists, believing that God is the highest Being, omnipotent and omnipresent.

Hamer, however, felt that she existed in the limbo of doubt – the "grand perhaps". She felt she was in the no-man's-land, between the certainties of believers and atheists, many of whom struck her as crusaders dedicated to annihilating the opposition.

I, too, exist in the limbo of doubt. Perhaps I internalise the idea of God as inward reality – the "still small voice" and the symbol of the noblest visions and ethical aspirations: the metric with which we measure our moral progress. It is an internal spiritual power, as opposed to an external, supranatural power.

I myself am never entirely comfortable to think of God as the source of all being – the creator of the universe, because this seems to me to be a materialistic, rather than a spiritual or even an ethical, concept. The philosopher, Bertrand Russell, expressed the futility of speculating on non-provable assertions such as a supernatural God who created the universe:

> *If I were to suggest that between the Earth and Mars there is a china teapot revolving about the sun in an elliptical orbit, nobody would be able to disprove my assertion, provided I were careful to add that the teapot is too small to be revealed even by our most powerful telescopes. But if I were to go on to say that, since my assertion cannot be disproved, it is intolerable presumption on the part of human reason to doubt it, I should rightly be thought to be talking nonsense.*
> (*Is there a God? Illustrated Magazine*, 1952 (unpublished))

That great poet and Anglican priest of the Welsh hills, R S Thomas, felt that it is easier to say what God is not, rather than what God is.

> *Why no! I never thought other than*
> *That God is that great absence*
> *In our lives, the empty silence*
> *Within, the place where we go*
> *Seeking, not in hope to*
> *Arrive or find.*

This is the concept of "Via Negativa" enunciated by St Thomas Aquinas in the thirteenth century. We must content ourselves with considering "the ways in which God does not exist, rather than the ways in which he does". As stated in Paul's second letter to the Corinthians:

> *We look not at the things which are seen, but at the things which are not seen, for the things which are seen are temporal; but the things which are not seen are eternal.*

If God is to be defined in terms of what he is not, then how are we to understand the role of Jesus Christ? The word "Christ" means "The Anointed One" who is the saviour and redeemer of the Jewish people, and mankind as a whole. But who was he? <u>The</u> Son of God – or <u>a</u> son of God?

Do we have to apply a theological DNA test to determine his paternity? Can he be the son of the unknown? Was he a healer, a magician, a prophet, a teacher, a political reformer, the saviour of the world, the Messiah?

That Unitarian deep thinker, Revd Cliff Reed, regards Jesus as a man and a religious symbol who is constantly gnawing away at our collective and individual consciousness. But what if we strip away the supernatural qualities of Jesus Christ – born of a virgin, walking on water, raising people from the dead, being resurrected and sitting on the right side of God? Christ then becomes human flesh. And what if we remove his spiritual power as a saviour and redeemer of mankind? We then take the Christ out of Jesus Christ and are left with the man Jesus: a teacher and practitioner of supreme, sublime, universal love. We then, perhaps, have moved from Christian belief to religious humanism, both of which straddle contemporary Unitarianism. This was dangerous thinking before the Reformation: in 1529, Ludwig Haetzer was beheaded for believing that Jesus was a leader and teacher who should not be worshipped as divine.

The Unitarian minister, Revd Anthony Howe, looks at the issue differently, and from a more Christian perspective. He says that when he looks at Jesus he is not, in fact, seeing God. Instead, he sees a reflection of God – perhaps a perfect reflection – and in this sense he sees Jesus as divine:

> *What I deny is the deity of Jesus. I don't believe Jesus is God. This is why, among other reasons, I'm a Unitarian.*
>
> *In Jesus, I see the Christ, the anointed, the chosen. When I say that, I mean that I draw a distinction between the human Jesus and the Christ.*
>
> *How do I do this? Well, by saying that Jesus is the man, and Christ is who he was called to be. Jesus is the human, Christ is the divine calling and promise that worked within him – and in Jesus these two things, for me, seem inseparable.*

The Carmelite nun and mystic, St. Theresa of Avila, saw a strong connection between ourselves and Christ. We have the power to reflect his compassion and continue his good works. We can be his instruments on earth:

> *Christ has no body now on earth but yours, no hands, no feet but yours. Yours are the eyes with which Christ looks out his compassion to the world. Yours are the feet with which he is to go about doing good. Yours are the hands with which he is to bless us now.*

The German philosopher Friedrich Nietzsche, however, announced to the world that "God is dead". His existentialist parable, *The Madman,* was about a man who ran to the market place and cried incessantly: "I seek God! I seek God!" As many of those who did not believe in God were standing around just then, he provoked much laughter. The madman jumped into their midst and pierced them with his eyes.

> *Whither is God? I will tell you. We have killed him -- you and I. All of us are his murderers. But how did we do this? What were we doing when we unchained this earth from its sun? Whither is it moving now? Whither are we moving? Away from all suns?.... Do we not need to light lanterns in the morning? Do we hear nothing as yet of the noise of the gravediggers who are burying God? Do we smell nothing as yet of the divine decomposition? Gods, too, decompose. God is dead. God remains dead. And we have killed him.*

He asked the crowd how should they comfort themselves as the "murderers of the holiest and mightiest of all that the world has yet owned?" Who would wipe the blood off our knives, he asked, and "must we ourselves not become gods simply to appear worthy of it?".

Here the madman fell silent and looked again at his listeners; and they, too, were silent and stared at him in astonishment. At last, he threw his lantern on the ground, and it broke into pieces and was extinguished. "I have come too early," he said then; "my time is not yet. This tremendous event is still on its way, still wandering; it has not yet reached the ears of men."

This is the God that had to be killed, because nobody should tolerate being made into a mere object of God's absolute knowledge and total control. The parable of the Madman casts us unceremoniously into an existentialist void. Nietzsche warns us that:

When one gives up the Christian faith, one pulls the right to Christian morality out from under one's feet. This morality is by no means self-evident... By breaking one main concept out of Christianity, the faith in God, one breaks the whole: nothing necessary remains in one's hands.

But Nietzsche's death notice is of the passing of a supernatural being of a past age. It is not the poet RS Thomas's living God, which is intrinsically linked to nature.

It is alive. It is you,
God. Looking out I can see
no death......

There is nothing too ample
for you to overflow, nothing
so small that your workmanship
is not revealed.

For five thousand years or more, God looked down upon his people, be they his tribe, his nation, or all the inhabitants of the world, for, as the human concept of God grew larger, so did his domain. Living in a celestial world high above the Earth, he answered some people's prayers and chastised others and was misused to justify religious and political autocracy and intolerance. This view of God began to fall apart when enlightened human beings began to look with a more critical eye at the creation of an expanding observable universe, of which they were a unique, yet diminishing, part.

The theologian Don Cupitt of the Sea of Faith movement believes that the question of whether God exists outside the religious requirement is of no religious interest. To him, religious faith is merely a human construct. Perhaps the link between humans and God is simply love:

God is love; and he that dwelleth in love dwelleth in God, and God in him (John 4.16).

That love can be understood in the life and teachings of Jesus. But first we need to separate Jesus from the uncomfortable history of the Christian church; from the Crusades and Inquisitions to colonialism led by the bullet and the Bible. It is a legacy which disfigured the Christianity embarked on in His name. To understand the authentic Jesus, perhaps we need to end our obsession with his crucifixion and not roll the boulder from his tomb. In the words of the Unitarian minister, Revd Sarah Tinker:

> *This Jesus stands apart from the violent manner of his death and the church doctrines that arose from it. Resurrection and atonement of sins are not a theology that speaks to me. But what does speak loud and clearly is Jesus' mythic quality, combined with his earthly reality, this inspirational being, who left us a hugely potent legacy contained in fragments of text, reminding us, again and again, of the power of love.*

Radical Christians perhaps should develop an unselfish and disinterested love of their fellow beings, a love that does not ask for anything in return. Good actions can no longer be performed because we know that God is watching what we do or because we expect rewards in heaven. We must strive to attain a spiritual consciousness, because in doing so we lose the old ego, the part of us that fears death. As Cupitt says:

> *Quickly we must die to death, escape from this natural ego that clings so hopelessly to life, and enter upon a new life and divine form of consciousness disinterested, universal, no-egoistical and free.*

And in the words of the theologian, Trevor Greenfield:

> *As the pillars of heaven are torn down, then God, and perhaps more significantly, Jesus, fall to Earth, with God subsumed within the process of history and Jesus recognised as an inspired but ultimately human teacher.*

The conundrum is that Christian orthodoxy proclaims Christ as God Incarnate. It is an aspect of an essentially Trinitarian God who took human form to effect the salvation of humankind but, while doing so, remained uniquely God. Perhaps this conundrum is exemplified in the crucifixion of Jesus:

> *From the sixth hour until the ninth hour, a darkness came over all the land. And then Jesus cried out in a loud voice "My God, My God, why have you forsaken me?"*

If Jesus was part of an all-knowing, all-loving, Godhead, why should he fear abandonment? Could this in fact be Jesus, the human, in despair, asking himself why humankind has forsaken the path to universal love and moral perfection? Is this what we should be thinking as we look up at the cross, as opposed to feeling guilty for his supreme sacrifice for our sins?

Pastor Dietrich Bonhoeffer, in a letter written in prison before he was hanged by the Nazis, talks of moral perfection:

> *Encounter with Jesus Christ the experience that a transformation of all human life is given in the fact that "Jesus is there only for others".*
>
> *His "being there for others" is the experience of transcendence. It is only his being there for others, maintained till death, that is the ground of his omnipotence, omniscience and omnipresence.*

So perhaps we all have a choice: between a supernatural Christ sitting at the right hand of a supernatural God whom we worship, and the sublime teacher of universal love, Jesus, sitting at *our* right side, whom we struggle to follow.

Can God's grave diggers proclaim a Godless morality? Let me end with the words of Richard Holloway, former Primus of the Episcopal Church of Scotland:

> *If there is that which we call God, and God is more than the projection of our own best values and longing for transcendence, then God must be involved in all our moral struggles, ...so that the attempt by humans to discover a morality apart from God might, paradoxically, be God's greatest triumph; and our attempt to live morally as though there were no God might be the final test of faith.*

The supernatural God is dead. Long live God – the love in Jesus, and the love of God in all of us.

Sources cited in this chapter

Dietrich Bonhoeffer, *Letters and Papers from Prison*. SCM Press, 1981.

Don Cupitt. *The Sea of Faith: Christianity in Change*. BBC, 1984.

Corinthians 2. 4:18.

Trevor Greenfield. *An Introduction to Radical Theology: The Death and Resurrection of God*. O Books, 2006.

Margaret Hamer. *Unitarian Views of God*. General Assembly of Unitarian and Free Christian Churches, 2010.

Richard Holloway. *Leaving Alexandria: A Memoir of Faith and Doubt*. Canongate, 2012.

Antony Howe. *Unitarian Views of Jesus*. General Assembly of Unitarian and Free Christian Churches, 2009.

Friedrich Nietzsche, "The Madman", Gay Science, para.125 (1882, 1887), in *The Portable Nietzsche*, trans. Walter Kaufmann. Viking, 1954.

R.S. Thomas. *Collected Poems: 1945–1990*. Phoenix, 1993.

Sarah Tinker. *Unitarian Views of Jesus*. General Assembly of Unitarian and Free Christian Churches, 2009.

3 Turning the Tide of Faith

The Sea of Faith
Was one, too, at the full, and round earth's shore
Lay like the folds of a bright girdle furled.
But now I only hear
Its melancholy, long, withdrawing roar,
Retreating, to the breath
Of the night-wind, down the vast edges drear
And naked shingles of the world.
(Matthew Arnold)

The sea in Arnold's poem *Dover Beach* is a metaphor for established religion. Its certainty was withdrawing itself from human grasp during the mid-nineteenth century, when the poem was written. The supernatural world was slowly and inexorably slipping away. "The Sea of Faith" was receding like the ebbing tide, leaving us on "a darkling plain". The world which "seems to lie before us like a land of dreams, so various, so beautiful, so new, hath really neither joy, nor love, nor light, nor certitude, nor peace, nor help for pain".

The radical theologian, Don Cupitt, appropriated *The Sea of Faith* for the title for his ground-breaking book based on his TV series. It argued that the melancholy retreat of the old tide need not lead to an existential darkness. A new tide can begin to flow. Religion can free itself from the straitjacket of its outworn beliefs. Christianity should now be practised without dogma, as a spiritual path, an ethic, and an authentic way of giving meaning to life. In many ways, this 'Sea of Faith' movement is congruent with mainstream Unitarian thought.

For about two millennia, roughly between 500 BCE to AD 1500, much religious thought and action as dictated by the established Roman Catholic Church was dominated by a stark contrast between the fleeting wretched world below, in which we are consigned to spend our brief lives, and the eternal heavenly world above, which is the soul's true home. This earthly world was seen as merely a state of probation during which the soul prepared itself for the life to come. All norms of thought and action were located in the supernatural world; religious attention was concentrated on it, and religious action was understood as being traffic with it. The world of the dead and of heavenly beings was immensely more "real" than this earthly world. It was thus important to assist souls in purgatory with masses, indulgences, and prayers, and to invoke the intercession of the saints. Belief in life after death was strong, because the whole orientation of religion was towards the supernatural world above. It was essentially an metaphysical view.

By undergoing the rite of baptism, one put oneself irrevocably under the Church's jurisdiction for life. Anyone who departed from this "true faith" threatened the foundations of society and deserved punishment as a heretic. This doctrinaire view led to the Church believing that the other Abrahamic faiths were invalid -- as were Eastern religions such as Hinduism and philosophies such as Confucianism and Buddhism. Indeed, in 1704 Pope Clement XI condemned Confucianism as atheistic; leading the Chinese Emperor K'ang-Hsi to forbid his subjects to practise Christianity. So, ironically, the chance to evangelise China was lost.

As the frontiers of knowledge were pushed forward, the Catholic Church tried to resist new scientific thinking. In 1609, the Church found Galileo "vehemently suspect of heresy" for holding the opinion that it is the sun, and not the earth, that lies at the centre of the universe. This apparently diminished the status of God as the centre of the universe. So, Galileo was required to "abjure, curse and detest" those opinions and was sentenced by the Inquisition to house arrest for the rest of his life. Almost four centuries later, the Vatican Curia issued a statement to the effect that he was in fact correct. Better late than never.

A similar reaction to scientific knowledge was the Anglican Church's rejection of Darwin's *On the Origin of Species,* since it undermined the story of Creation as told in the *Book of Genesis.* Darwin just couldn't Adam and Eve it. One of the most heated exchanges concerning his theory took place in 1860 during a debate at Oxford University's Museum of Natural History. The Bishop of Oxford, "Soapy Sam" Wilberforce, asked Darwin's fellow evolutionist, Thomas Huxley, whether it was through his grandfather or his grandmother that he claimed to be descended from a monkey. Huxley replied that he would not be ashamed to have an ape for his ancestor, but he would be ashamed to be associated with a cleric who used his intellectual gifts to obscure the truth. At which point, a lady fainted and had to be carried out of the museum.

These radicals were not Dawkins-like atheists intent on debunking religion. Galileo was a friend of Pope Urban VIII. Darwin, whose family were free-thinking Unitarians, considered it "absurd to doubt that a man [sic] might be an ardent theist as well as an evolutionist". All that these scientists were doing was pushing forward the frontiers of knowledge of the material world.

If traditional theology had not been predicated on this supernatural view of the world, a less conflictual discourse could have led to a more natural turning of the tide, avoiding many people being trapped on the naked shingles of secularism.

Over the centuries, this metaphysical view of the world provoked a reaction. The modern secularism saw the world in nihilistic terms. The nineteenth-century philosopher, Arthur Schopenhauer, put humans firmly in their place in this world:

> *In endless space, countless luminous spheres, round each of which some dozen smaller spheres revolve, hot at the core and covered with a cold hard crust; on this crust a mouldy film has produced living knowing beings.*

So, we are like corks bobbing on the ocean, and our consciousness is a temporal by-product: the mere tool of an eternal and irresistible striving force that Schopenhauer calls "the Will". Even he would have been amazed at the vastness of the universe that we know of today.

For the poet, Friedrich Schiller, the importance of the individual is much diminished:

> *Chained to a single fragment of the whole, a human develops into nothing but a fragment; everlasting in his [sic] ear the monotonous sound of the wheel he turns, he never develops the harmony of his being; instead of putting the stamp of humanity upon his own nature, he becomes nothing more than the imprint of his occupation or his specialised knowledge.*

Don Cupitt. *The Sea of Faith: Christianity in Change*. BBC, 1984.

Sigmund Freud saw the old kind of religion used as a tool by an authoritarian society to persuade or coerce the individual into accepting the demands of culture. Karl Marx famously stated that religion was "the sigh of the oppressed creature, the feeling of a heartless world, the soul of soulless conditions, the opium of the people". Both, however, failed to foresee that in modern conditions religion can play a quite different role. The established church, of course, was used to give spurious authority to Fascist regimes such as Franco's Spain; but bottom–up religion was also used in the struggle against totalitarianism, as was Liberation Theology in South America (see chapter 12).

The nineteenth-century philosopher, Friedrich Nietzsche, is famous for his announcement that God is dead and that we have killed him (see Chapter 2). He argued that for there to be a religion there must be faith; and for there to be faith there must be assent to dogma: belief in some absolute metaphysical reality "out there".

Yet the existence of a non-creedal religion such as Unitarianism disproves this hypothesis. Most Unitarians – including those Unitarians who would describe themselves as Christians – would accept the death of metaphysics. Many would describe their faith as not assenting to outworn dogmas but as a commitment to living an authentic life, guided by the Golden Rule of doing to others as you would to yourself. Those ideals derive from the teachings of spiritual leaders such as Jesus Christ, as well as teachers from other religion traditions. Schopenhauer tells us:

> *... the weak point of all religions remains that they can never dare to confess to being allegorical, so that they have to present their doctrines in all seriousness as true: which, because of the absurdities essential to the allegory, leads to perpetual deception and a great disadvantage for religion.*
>
> Don Cupitt. *The Sea of Faith: Christianity in Change*. BBC, 1984.

In order to be a Christian, does one really have to believe in the Virgin birth, Christ's miracles, and his physical resurrection from the dead? If these so-called facts were proved not to be true, then would millions of people over the ages have worshipped Christ as God's only Son?

The Unitarian minister, David Usher, once mused that the teachings and deeds of Jesus would be even more miraculous if he had been a human being just like us, as opposed to a terrestrial visitant with supernatural powers.

That is why people like myself rejected Christianity at a very early age. At my confirmation, the Bishop of Liverpool never told me, *sotto voce,* that all these miracles were really allegories. To me, The Trinity became a metaphysical irrelevance that has perpetually distorted my view of Jesus Christ and his father – a cosmic Father Christmas or an authoritarian celestial ruler. Nor could I forget the Holy Ghost, who was always lurking in the background. Yet these images that were imprinted on my imagination so many years ago have not completely faded away with age. For to completely discard this metaphysical mantle can leave us naked and vulnerable to an existential world. We, mere humans, will always want to see a flag flying overhead and be tempted to muster around it – not caring what particular emblems are embroidered on it: the cross, the star of David, the crescent, or the hammer and sickle.

So, what image should we have of God? Well, perhaps none. We need to realise that God is the unknowable – in the words of the Victorian hymn, “immortal, invisible, God only wise”. But with our limited imagination we cannot envisage God as invisible. So, like the Invisible Man in the 1930s film, we need to wrap him up in bandages before we can believe that he is invisible. We need to understand that the eye with which He looks at us is simply the eye with which we look at Him. Religious ideas are inescapably, and rightly, human. They should not be used to describe God, but simply to liberate the spirit.

Even in ancient times, some religious thinkers had already grasped that all language about God is metaphorical or symbolic; that all religious ideas spring from humankind, even those carved in tablets of stone. If the concepts were not personified, they would be as difficult to decipher as the hieroglyphs on the Rosetta Stone. So, our religious imagery must be grounded in human authenticity if it is to relate to us and guide our behaviour throughout our lives.

C. S. Lewis has stated that when first thinking about God, we need to empty our minds of misconceptions. Then we must refill them with the truth about God - untainted by mythology, bad analogies or false mind pictures.

The image of God as a heavenly father is an anthropomorphic conception; whereas there is also a God beyond that God, unimaginable in both form and time. The imagined God that we carry about with us inclines us to behave as if an unseen, paternal eye watches over us. So, we form the habit of loving our neighbour as ourselves and acting as individuals who have something to live up to. Thus, religion has to be merely human in order to work as religion: a paradox that brings religion to within a hairsbreadth of secular humanism. The philosopher, Ludwig Wittgenstein, expresses it as thus:

> *An honest religious thinker is like a tightrope walker. He [sic] almost looks as though he were walking on nothing but air. His support is the slenderest imaginable. And yet it really is possible to walk on it.*
> Don Cupitt. *The Sea of Faith: Christianity in Change.* BBC, 1984.

This is a tightrope that some Unitarians have to walk on. We find it difficult to tread the rope of religious humanism without a metaphysical safety harness to avoid falling into the dark chasm of atheism or nihilism. In the words of Cupitt:

> *God is the sum of our values, representing to us their ideal unity... Values don't have to be independently and objectively existent beings in order to be able to claim our allegiance.*

Indeed, thinking of values as objective beings "out there" does not help us in any way to progress towards a clearer understanding of the special part that they play in our lives. As Cupitt continues:

> *The view that religious belief consists in holding a number of picturesque supernatural positions is encouraged by the continuing grip on people's minds of a decadent and mystifying dogmatic theology. In effect, I am arguing that it should be discarded entirely and replaced by the practice of religion – ethics and spirituality – and the philosophy of religion. Then religion will become itself again, with a clear intellectual conscience at last.*

He argues that the believer must "learn to recognise the imperfection and inadequacy of all human religious ideas and to follow an inner path of renunciation and progressive purging of illusions". But the historic task of religion – of embodying our values, witnessing to them, conserving them, setting them forth in symbols and securing their realisation in human life – remains unchanged. It will be performed all the better after the painted veil of illusion that has hitherto hidden its workings has finally dropped away.

The metaphysical God in his mechanical universe may be dead, and there are still those who place wreaths on his headstone. But we need to end this mourning and, perhaps, go through an existentialist stage, emerging into a religious life which is authentic to us and reflects our personal values. To remake God will be a slow and painful process, but it could lead to our very own resurrection. The second-century Christian, Hippolytus of Rome, even called on us to:

> *Abandon the search for God and the creation and other matters of a similar sort. Look for him by taking yourself as a starting point. Learn what is within you. Learn the sources of sorrow, joy, love and hate. If you complete these matters, you will find God in yourself.*

Swami Vivekananda (1863–1902) was the first Hindu missionary to the Western world. He spread the view, based on Vedantic teaching, that all religions are one. Their true followers tread different paths, but the paths lead to the same destination: the union (and, indeed, the identity) of the soul with God. He rejected the Christian idea of sin and taught that by living a virtuous life you can realise God in yourself:

> *When we have nobody to grope towards, no devil to blame, no personal God to carry our burdens, when we are alone responsible, then we shall rise to our highest and our best.*

Don Cupitt. *The Sea of Faith: Christianity in Change*. BBC, 1984.

The fourteenth-century Sufi poet, Hafiz, warned that "the great religions of the world are the ships ... and every sane person I know has jumped overboard". Free-thinkers such as Unitarians need to crew the lifeboats.

Sources cited in this chapter

Don Cupitt. *The Sea of Faith: Christianity in Change*. BBC, 1984.

Arthur Schopenhauer. *The World as Will and as Idea*. 1818.

Swami Vivekananda. *The Complete Works of Swami Vivekananda*. Advaita Ashrama, 1963.

4 Praying to Ourselves

My prayers must meet a brazen heaven
and fail and scatter all away ...
(Gerard Manley Hopkins)

Prayer is central to most religions, and it is much more than a ritual. Perhaps it is when you talk to God as opposed to meditation when you listen to God. There are two major types of prayer – petitionary and intercessional – and perhaps intercessional is the one more practised by us Unitarians. The ways in which prayer is practised are very varied, from the whirling dervishes of the Sufis to the silent prayer of the Quakers.

I am reminded of a story about intercessional prayer told to me by a wonderful Unitarian minister, the late Brian Anderson. For most of his life, Brian was an Anglican monk whose life was guided by prayerfulness. His true story was that of a "grand dame" who was laid up in St Thomas' Hospital – in a private suite, of course. She was visited by the humble hospital chaplain who asked her whether she would like him to pray for her. "Please don't bother, dear", she told him dismissively. "You see, the Dean has promised that next week he will pray for me in no less a place than Westminster Abbey." Would a dean's prayer rise further than a chaplain's, I wonder? How about that of a Unitarian minister? Let us not go there!

For most of my adult life I rejected prayer as irrational and even selfish. I suppose what I was really rejecting was petitionary prayer. Kneeling at the foot of the bed as a child, pretending to pray for forgiveness for a minor transgression at Christmas time but sneaking in a request for toys. I will always remember my next-door neighbour in Liverpool – a devout Irish Roman Catholic – confiding in me that she had prayed that my twin brother and I would pass the dreaded Eleven Plus exam. Sure enough, two months later a miracle happened – more astounding than the turning of water into wine. I actually passed! But my brother didn't. I'm sure Mrs Mulholland sent up prayers for both of us, but one prayer somehow must have got lost on the way.

An amusing story of the emptiness of such a prayer is one told by Anthony De Mello, an Indian Jesuit priest. Two boys on the way back from church were being pursued across a field by an angry bull. They were not going to make it over the nearest gate. One of the lads shouted "Nothing can save us save a quick prayer". In panic, the other one replied, "Well, I'll say one that my father says before meals: For what we are about to receive, Lord, make us truly grateful!".

Much more seriously, millions of prayers must have been uttered by Jews and others on their way to concentration camps or lined up in front of the gas chambers. Were their prayers not good enough – not loud enough to be heard by God? Or were they, in the words of the Jesuit priest and poet, Gerard Manley Hopkins, prayers that "meet a brazen heaven and fail and scatter all away":

I cannot buoy my heart above.
Above I cannot entrance win.
I feel the long success of sin.
I reckon precedents of love,
But feel the long success of sin.

The poet, R S Thomas, also felt this overwhelming frustration when he knelt before the altar in a Welsh church. As an Anglican priest, he waits for God to speak and yet he feels he has been unable to intercede with God on behalf of his expectant congregation:

All that close throng
Of spirits waiting, as I,
For the message.
Prompt me, God;
But not yet. When I speak,
Though it be you who speak
Through me, something is lost.
The meaning is in the waiting.

The focus of many intercessional prayers is on restoring an individual's health. You can see them written on cards in many churches. But there is little empirical evidence that intercessional prayer actually has much effect. An experiment conducted by an American cardiologist on patients recovering from heart operations found no difference in the medical outcomes between those patients who were prayed for by a congregation and those who were not. Furthermore, those who knew that they had been prayed for actually suffered significantly more medical complications than those who didn't know that they were being prayed for. Was God being perverse, or did the patients who knew that they were being prayed for by complete strangers suffer the additional stress of mistakenly believing that they were on their last legs? And would the results have been reversed if they had thought that the prayers had been sent up by their loved ones rather than by strangers? There are, however, studies that have found that petitionary prayers uttered by patients themselves may have some therapeutic effect on their mental health, particularly for those who are depressed about their physical condition. An article in the *British Medical Journal* in 1910 opined:

> *It is unquestionable that prayer, inspired by living faith, is a force acting within the patient, which places him [sic] in the most favourable condition for the stirring of the pool of hope that lies, still and hidden, it may be, in the depths of human nature.*

I often see standard petitionary prayers printed in *The Liverpool Echo*. They are published by the Roman Catholic Church for the use of worshippers in times of need. One is addressed to the "most beautiful flower of Mount Carmel, Immaculate Virgin, Mother of God". The petitioners have to pray for three days using the required rubric, and setting out their personal cause or petition. They have to repeat three times "Pray for us who have who have recourse to thee ... Holy Mary, I place this cause in your hands"; then, abracadabra, the request will be granted – and then the prayer needs to be published. Presumably if the request is not granted then it is not published. So, it's a "win–win" result for the efficacy of petitionary prayer.

What then of the efficacy of praying for refugees in a war zone, or for the world's poor? Can God replenish the empty belly of Africa as we mouth our prayers at Lent? The theologian and nonconforming Methodist minister, Dr Leslie Weatherhead, has stated that such prayers are valuable in raising empathy concerning the plight of fellow beings, but they are too full of expectancy to be of any practical value for the prayed-for.

Prayer can be difficult for some Unitarians, particularly in the absence of a personal God – although I am sure that some of us pray for a sermon to end. Do we Unitarians address our prayers to God, or to the Divine Spirit, or to the Nameless One? And if you post a letter addressed to "whom it may concern" are you ever likely to get a reply?

The anti-theist, Christopher Hitchens, has remarked that the person who prays is the one who thinks that God has arranged matters all wrong but who thinks that he can instruct God to put them right. In the words of Kahlil Gibran in *The Prophet*:

> *We cannot ask thee for aught, for thou knowest our needs before they are born in us.*

So, perhaps, we need to widen the purpose and nature of prayer rather than merely mock it. The existentialist philosopher, Kierkegaard, stated that "the function of prayer is not to influence God, but, rather, to change the nature of the one that prays".

Maybe our most effective prayers are those that ask for nothing, but help us communicate with each other. They don't depend on a supernatural intervention – a divine waving of a magic wand that will give us what we want, whether a toy for a child or a Jew's release from a concentration camp.

Perhaps God does not intervene tangibly in human affairs. Perhaps, we ourselves are God's hands – not in his hands. To quote Gibran again:

> *God listens not to your words save when He Himself utters them through your lips.*

Maybe prayer can be personally transformative rather than a petition to change external circumstances. Buddhists do not pray to an external God but contemplate or meditate to awaken their own spiritual enlightenment, buried deep within them. Even for Christians, it does not just require kneeling on a hassock. It is all about exposure and surrender to an outer Being. As the Christian missionary, Florence Allshorn, once said:

> *Just lying in the sun doing nothing, surrendering your body to it, the sun blazing down on you, affects your body and your senses, so this surrendering to that transforming Power affects the soul, and I believe that as truly as the sun changes the colour of your skin, so that Power changes you at the centre.*

Gibran observes that we pray in our distress and in our need. Prayer is "the expansion of yourself into the living ether". If we are to open ourselves to the transforming powers of God's presence, then we are going to have to listen – not just make requests.

By learning to listen to that inner voice, we have taken a big step spiritually; but we also need to act on that voice, individually and collectively. For communal prayer is very important in centering our thoughts, listening to our inner voice, and joining up our acts of loving kindness. In Gibran's words:

> *When you pray, you rise to meet in the air those who are praying at that very hour, and whom save in a prayer you may not meet.*

Weatherhead feels that he is praying for a fellow human when he meets him or her, and "we open our hearts to one another on what I want to call 'the God level'". To open oneself unconditionally in love is to be with that person in the presence of God, and that is what Whitehead sees as the heart of intercession.

> *To pray for another is to expose both oneself and him [sic] to the common ground of our being; it is to see one's concern for him in terms of ultimate concern, to let God into the relationship. Intercession is to be with another at that depth, whether in silence or compassion or action. It may consist simply in listening, when we take the otherness of the other person most seriously.... It may not be specifically religious, it may not be consciously Christian: but may be a meeting of Christ in that man, because his humanity is accepted without any reservations.*

That should be the aim of a free-thinking, religious community like ours. It was beautifully expressed in the words of the late Unitarian minister, David Monk:

> *Prayer is the practice of placing attention on a Presence which permeates and inspires the minds and hearts of a congregation who join together in worship and celebration. The purpose of prayer is to raise our consciousness and open our hearts to the transforming power of that Presence, so that throughout the period of communal worship we are released from the mundane preoccupations of ordinary life and experience a level of awareness, or way of being, that transcends the individual self, which binds us together in fellowship, expands and deepens our awareness of ourselves, of those we are with, and of the world in which we live.*

Sources cited in this chapter

Kahlil Gibran. *The Prophet*. William Heinemann, 1980.

J. H. Oldham, *Florence Allshorn*. Student Christian Movement Press. 1955.

R S Thomas. *Collected Poems: 1945–1990*. Phoenix, 1993.

Leslie Weatherhead. *The Christian Agnostic*. Hodder and Stoughton, 1965.

5 Living, Loving, and Dying

The danger of religion lies in its claim to absolute immutable moral knowledge which, if justified, would indeed give its adherents a special place in instructing others how to behave, perhaps even a right to do so. (Mary Warnock)

The state and society are constantly imposing norms on all of us. We need to examine the role and justification of religion's involvement in moral and legal matters: the right to life, the right to choose whom we love, and the right to die. Religion has underpinned our morality for centuries, but the question to be asked is whether in a much more secular society (with only a third believing in a God and according to a YouGov poll), we need to begin to prise it from the grip of politics and the law. Many of these issues are raised by the philosopher, Mary Warnock, in her book *Dishonest to God: On Keeping Religion out of Politics*. The Victorian Utilitarian and Liberal John Stuart Mill felt that the role of the state should not be to enforce conventional morality. This concept was developed by the legal philosopher H L A Hart in his seminal work *Law, Liberty and Morality*. It stated that the law had no business in interfering with private acts that harmed no-one; providing the intellectual reasoning for law reform in the 1960s on homosexuality and abortion.

No one doubts the pre-eminent role played by Christian religion in British society down the ages. It is even institutionalised – with the role of the monarch as the head of the Anglican Church and the right of senior Anglican bishops to sit on the House of Lords benches. The Prime Minister even has the right to make the final choice of whom to appoint as Archbishop of Canterbury. In 1928, Parliament actually rejected the Church of England's proposed revisions to the *Book of Common Prayer*. The influence of both the Anglican and Roman Catholic Churches over children's education is considerable; one third of schools within the state education system are denominational. In 2011, the then Tory Education Secretary, Michael Gove, even issued a bound copy of the King James Bible to every primary school to coincide with its 400th anniversary. Most gathered dust, but some might have been useful as door stops.

Sixteenth-century common law required and empowered the state to defend Christianity. Miscreants who insulted Jesus Christ could be hanged. The last successful private blasphemy prosecution for blasphemous libel was initiated in 1977 by Mary Whitehouse, a teacher and Christian crusader. *Gay News* had published James Kirkup's poem "*The Love that Dares to Speak its Name*". It described a gay centurion engaging in sexual activity with the dead body of Christ. The editor, Denis Lemon, was fined £500 and given a suspended sentence of nine months' imprisonment. Such religious obscenity would definitely have offended Christians – but so would Richard Dawkins' pronouncements that God did not exist. It all seemed rather irrelevant, since Lemon was anyway likely to be burnt in Hell's fiery furnace for eternity. It was only in 2008 that the blasphemy law was abolished.

But no one doubts that the Christian religion has now lost its dominant influence over our everyday lives. Many are unaware of the tenets in the Bible, and fewer and fewer attend church, except for rites of passage. Do not be deceived by young people's incessant cries of "Oh my God!". Those are not exhortations to their creator.

I am not suggesting that religion should curl up and die in a ditch, as desired by Dawkins. What is needed in the 21st century is getting the right balance right between religion, morality, and human rights under the law. Private morality that is dictated by religious conscience should not determine public policy. Democracy must always predominate over theocracy.

Perhaps one of the most important issues confronting the established churches is the right to life. Jacob Rees-Mogg, the politician who makes Benjamin Disraeli seem positively hip, made a recent statement on abortion that most people recoiled at:

> *Abortion is morally indefensible. Life is sacrosanct and begins at the point of conception. I am therefore completely opposed to abortion, including conceptions resulting from rape or incest.*

Yet, he was merely faithfully repeating the official tenet of the Roman Catholic Church, as set out in its catechism. So, it is to the church that any opprobrium should be directed – not to an individual, albeit zealous, member of the faith. Yet, as few as one in fourteen British Catholics accept their church's teaching that abortion should not be allowed in any circumstances. Of course, the high level of abortions in the UK is disturbing, and many perhaps could be avoided by a greater use of contraception. But this too is forbidden by the church, on the grounds that it is an impediment to true marital love. In the words of Pope John Paul II:

> *For those who are filled with the Holy Spirit, contraception is simply unthinkable. They know it replaces the true language of the body with a lie. And lying within the heart of marital intimacy has a ripple effect, as does speaking the truth. Spouses who strive to speak honestly in the nuptial embrace also strive to be open and honest with each other in the other areas of their married life.*

I well remember my next-door neighbour in Liverpool being told by doctors that because of her heart defect her life would be imperilled if she had another child. So, she had to go to the priest for special dispensation to use contraception. In other words, she had to seek permission from the Church to "nuptially embrace" her husband without the fear of dying! Furthermore, the Roman Catholic Church got the moral choice facing African Catholics badly wrong when it ruled that the risk of dying from full-blown AIDS was the least-bad alternative to the use of contraceptives.

Another quandary for the established churches has been the right to love whom you please. Issues of sexual relations and sexuality have riven the Anglican Church. And yet I cannot see their relevance to theology, other than a line in the Old Testament written seven centuries before Christ: the infamous Book of Leviticus 18.22, which describes having sexual relations with another man as an "abomination". This is the same authority that punishes blasphemy through stoning and banning those reaping to the very edges of a field. It is more a question of church politics and social prejudices than a question of theology. Thank goodness that the Unitarian Church has not got into this bind. We were the first church to appoint openly gay clergy and to conduct same-sex blessings, well before the Marriage (Same Sex Couples) Act was introduced in 2013.

What is of even greater concern is the homophobic attitudes of the established churches. Remember the case of Rev. Jeffrey John. His nomination to the bishopric of Reading was overturned by conservative bishops on the grounds that he was in a loving (yet celibate) relationship with another C of E priest. He was, however, subsequently appointed to be Dean of St Albans. So, a gay dean is theologically permissible but not a gay bishop! You can be a very reverend gay but not a right reverend gay. You couldn't make it up!

The Church of England has been accused of inconsistency in its attempts to reconcile traditional teachings on sexuality with more liberal interpretations. Its current stance is that homosexual people can be priests but must remain celibate, because of the Bible's teaching on sex outside marriage. Yet, at the same time, the Church is officially opposed to allowing gay couples to marry – although some senior clerics are in favour. So, the only option open to Jeffrey John was to enter a civil partnership with his long-term partner, but to remain in a celibate relationship. Presumably, their bedroom has CCTV linked to Lambeth Palace.

In its official response to the Government's consultation on same-sex marriage, the Church of England even suggested that the move could open the way to the disestablishment of the Church. Dr John has said:

> *If you are gay, please don't judge God by the Church. The Church is meant to show Christ's face to the world and on this subject, it doesn't... If you are gay, then please understand that God made you as you are, and loves you as you are, and if you invite him into your relationship, then of course he will bless you and sustain your love just as much as he blesses and sustains any other marriage.*

There has always been deep-rooted sexism in the established churches, again with little theological justification. It has reflected the patriarchal society down the ages. The Roman Catholic Church will not contemplate ordaining women priests. The Anglican Church reluctantly agreed to do so and it has now even managed to consecrate female bishops. Contrast this with our Unitarian churches, which began ordaining women ministers over a hundred years ago.

The Equality Bill that the Labour Government introduced in 2010 was pronounced by the Anglican Bishop of Durham as "erasing God from political life". Pope Benedict XVI agreed with him that it was a violation of natural law and demanded that religion must be brought back into British politics. All the Bill was intended to do was to tighten and clarify existing anti-discrimination law. Its most controversial clause would have made it clear that churches were exempt from anti-discrimination law in their appointment of strictly religious officials such as priests and bishops. There would, however, be no exemption if churches discriminated against women or gays or non-believers applying for non-secular positions such as vergers or gardeners. This amendment was heavily defeated by the unelected House of Lords. To employ a verger or gardener who was gay or a member of another faith was seen as an assault on freedom of worship. This was nonsense on stilts, but the amendment was dropped by the government. It affected a relatively few jobs, but it symbolised a triumph of religion's supremacy over secular equality law: nonsense over rationality.

We now come to the thorny issue of the right to die. A YouGov poll in 2012 found that 82 per cent of Anglicans and 66 per cent of Catholics supported the notion of mentally competent individuals with incurable or terminal diseases who wish to end their lives receiving medical assistance to do so, without those assisting them facing prosecution.

Many suffering patients are in practice helped to a speedier death. Was it not Lord Dawson who hastened the death of a patient by injecting him with a lethal dose of morphine and cocaine? He administered it to King George the Fifth so that he could die "with the dignity and serenity which he so richly merited" and, most important, that the death could be announced the next morning in *The Times* as opposed to the evening rags. If the facts had been disclosed then Dawson could not just have been charged with euthanasia but presumably with high treason!

The Unitarian Church was the first denomination to take a positive stance on assisted dying. In 2013, the Unitarian General Assembly voted in favour of a motion supporting greater choice at the end of life. The motion called for legislation to provide the choice of assisted death to those facing an intolerable existence because of a debilitating and/or incurable condition. The law should "allow them compassionate assistance in achieving such a death without fear of the prosecution of anyone involved".

As a Samaritan, I often have to give emotional support – but never advice – to people who have suicidal thoughts or are even planning to end their life. A few of our callers are terminally ill, but most suicidal callers are suffering from deep depression and would not satisfy the criteria for assisted dying stipulated by the Unitarian motion. Samaritans have a duty to respect a caller's right to die – neither assisting or resisting their intention. Sometimes, the Samaritan volunteer is the last person "to hold the hand" of the caller as he or she departs this life.

The issue of assisted dying rests on two concepts: that of the sanctity of life, which is primarily a religious argument; and the principle of patient autonomy, which is the cornerstone of medical ethics. The Church of England House of Bishops, together with the Catholic Bishops' Conference, have stated that their arguments against assisted dying are based on their belief that God himself has given to humankind the gift of life. But should a non-believer who is terminally ill be prevented by religious-based law from opting for assisted suicide as opposed to palliative care in a hospice?

In one case, a woman, Diane Pretty, was suffering from Motor Neurone Disease and paralysed from the neck down. She wanted a legal assurance that her husband would not be prosecuted for assisting her to die. Such assurance never came. Her life came to an end with her being fed through a tube to her stomach. Conversely, the parents of an eight-month-old baby with genetic brain damage were told by a judge that their wish for their son to continue to be medically treated could no longer be respected: Great Ormond Street Hospital could lawfully withdraw all treatment save for palliative care to permit Charlie Gard to die with dignity.

Should indeed a Christian who was granted the wish to die have the right to a religious funeral? A 60-year-old from Rome who had been paralysed for two decades had been kept alive by a tube that pumped air into his lungs. Piergiorgio Welby had pleaded to be allowed to die and, in the end, his doctor turned off the pump. The Rome diocese, of which the Pope is bishop, then denied him a Catholic funeral. Hundreds attended his lay funeral in the piazza outside Welby's church. The response of Pope Benedict XVI was uncompromising: "We must accept life from its beginning to its natural sunset". On that day, the Church's compassion had sunk with the sun.

These are tortuously difficult ethical issues, and drafting legislation allowing dignity in dying but proscribing a licence to kill will not be easy. But it should be influenced not by any religious concept of the sanctity of life but by the principle of human compassion. Let me end by quoting Warnock:

> *The laws of God are in fact moral principles which may change over time and in some cases be flatly rejected. To regard such principles as the unique possession of people who hold certain metaphysical beliefs is to demean the status in society of people who do not hold such beliefs..... Morally speaking, believers and unbelievers are equal, and their right to make their voice heard democratically is equal. Democracy must always transcend theocracy.*

Sources cited in this chapter

Jeffrey John. *Permanent, Faithful, Stable: Christian Same-Sex Partnerships.* Darton, Longman and Todd Ltd, 1994.

Leviticus, chapter 18, verse 22.

Warnock, Mary. *Dishonest to God: On Keeping Religion out of Politics.* Continuum, 2010.

6 Jesus: left or right side of God?

> *Jesus was like some terrible moral huntsman digging mankind out of the snug burrows in which they had lived hitherto. In the white blaze of this kingdom of his there was to be no property, no privilege, no pride and precedence; no motive indeed and no reward but love.*
> (H. G. Wells)

The question of whether Jesus should sit on the left-hand side of God, as opposed to the right-hand side is, of course, a rhetorical one. It merely allows us to explore the complex relationship between politics and religion in the context of the UK. For many Unitarians, the teachings of Jesus are an exemplar of how we might live in this life – rather than a means by which we might purchase personal salvation in any after-life. Such teachings guide us through our personal lives, but they also influence our views on how society should develop ethically.

There is, however, often a nervousness about linking politics and religion, on the part of both politicians and clerics. There is a danger in both the politicisation of religion and the theologising of politics. The Christian Tory grandee Quintin Hogg (later Lord Hailsham) in his *Case for Conservatism* considered that when a politician turned to religion for legitimising purposes it was "an end of honest politics". It is ironic that while religion plays an important role in the politics of secular America, it now plays such an insignificant part in a state which has an established church. There is no bible belt in Britain. No prime minister has the temerity to proclaim "God bless Britain". Yet it was the liberal, progressive Archbishop of Canterbury, William Temple, who, in 1942, opined that "All the great political questions of our day are primarily theological". Almost sixty years later, his successor, Rowan Williams, supported this view:

> *Christian ethics is relentlessly political because it cannot be adequately expressed in terms of atomized rights vested in individuals or groups, but looks beyond to the kind of community in which free interaction for the sake of each other is made possible. That means adjustment and listening; it means politics.*

Christians can be found on both ends of the political spectrum, and Christianity has been both a progressive force and a conservative, though declining, force throughout our history. The historian, Eliza Filby, in her book *God and Mrs Thatcher*, offers an interesting insight into the Victorian era, when politics and religion were closely entwined. Parties and votes were sliced along denominational lines, with the Conservative Party firmly positioned as the protector of the Church of England, and the Liberal Party promoting the interests of the Nonconformists. Utilitarianism was a significant political and ethical philosophy in that era, pondering how to achieve the greatest happiness of the greatest number. It was not so much based on Christian ethics as developing a moral calculus of pleasure and pain. The prominent Utilitarian and Liberal, John Stuart Mill, held a firm belief in individual liberty: Parliament should legislate only to prohibit harm, not to enforce conventional morality. Nevertheless, he felt that such freedom could not be secured without a measure of limited state action, such as the provision of education, insurance against illness, and enforceable labour standards.

The end of that era ushered in a third party, the Labour Party. Its early values were based on Christian socialism: Harold Wilson proclaimed that its existence "owed more to Methodism than to Marxism". This chimed with the ethical socialist R. H. Tawney's axiom that "morality was superior to dogma". Tawney did not try to construct a political religion by fusing Christianity and socialism. He drew out the radical strands of the Gospel and hoped to persuade Christians to lean to the side of socialism without equating a socialist social order with the Kingdom of God. Labour's first leader, Keir Hardy, once described socialism as "the embodiment of Christianity in our industrial system". So, all the three parties could claim a Christian ethos and each continued to feed off its spiritual heritage.

Christianity, however, ceased to play a pivotal role in politics after the First World War. As Filby states, "disillusionment replaced faith as Britons dropped the cross somewhere amidst the muddy mass slaughter of the Somme". The ties between political parties and denominations loosened as class replaced religion as the central dividing line.

There was, however, a strong Christian ethical underpinning to the Attlee government's creation of the Welfare State. It was very much influenced by Tawney and the Liberal economist, William Beveridge, whose report was aimed at banishing poverty through universal benefits. Temple remarked that the Beveridge Report was "the first time anyone had set out to embody the whole spirit of the Christian ethic in an Act of Parliament".

Tawney, Beveridge, and Atlee learned their Christian social action from their volunteering at Toynbee Hall, rather than by reading biblical texts. It was a university settlement in the East End of London, established by a Victorian vicar. It brought potential leaders face to face with poverty, giving them the opportunity to develop solutions that they could take with them into national life. So that modest place had an indirect, but huge, influence on establishing the modern welfare state.

There was an attempted revival of religion in politics after the Swinging 1960s and turbulent 1970s. A small number of leading politicians entered public service with strong religious convictions, although the electorate as a whole had little interest in organised religion. The most important of these politicians was Margaret Thatcher, who was a committed Christian with strong non-conformist roots. She was greatly influenced by her grocer father, Alderman Alfred Roberts, who was a Methodist preacher at Grantham's Finkin Street Wesleyan Chapel.

Her conservatism was based on the Protestant work ethic, and values of thrift and piety. It was greatly influenced by Max Weber's *The Protestant Ethic and the Spirit of Capitalism,* which saw profit as an end in itself and its pursuit as virtuous. Market-driven capitalism was a major tenet of Protestantism. Filby, however, believes that Thatcher was uncomfortable with any association between the free market and a culture of unbridled greed, which "ran contrary to her own moral understanding of her political values". Her Grantham grocer father would have disapproved of the Yuppie culture. To quote her address to the Church of Scotland's Assembly in Edinburgh in May 1988, dubbed "The Sermon on the Mound":

> *We are told we must work and use our talents to create wealth...Indeed abundance rather than poverty has a legitimacy which derives from the very nature of Creation....But it is not the creation of wealth that is wrong but love of money for its own sake. The spiritual dimension comes in deciding what one does with the wealth.....any set of social*

and economic arrangements which is not founded on the acceptance of individual responsibility will do nothing but harm.

Thatcher stated that "Christianity is about spiritual redemption, not social reform", although she did recognise the role of the state in providing a safety net:

The only way we can ensure that no-one is left without sustenance, help or opportunity, is to have laws to provide for health and education, pensions for the elderly, succour for the sick and disabled. But intervention by the State must never become so great that it effectively removes personal responsibility.

At the other end of the political spectrum was the political dissenter and peace campaigner, Tony Benn. His inspiring force was his mother, Margaret Wedgwood Benn, who was a Biblical scholar and founder member of the League of the Church Militant, the predecessor of the Movement for the Ordination of Women. She would teach her young son that the story of the Bible was based on the struggle between "the Kings who had power, and the prophets who preached righteousness". Late in life, Benn described himself as a Christian atheist. He was unsure of the existence of God, but believed in "Jesus the prophet, not Christ the King", the historical Jesus, "the carpenter of Nazareth", who preached social justice and egalitarianism. His socialism owed much more to the teachings of Jesus, but without the mysteries within which they are presented, than it owed to the writings of Marx. Unlike Thatcher, Benn downplayed the importance of personal responsibility and emphasised the need for an ethical society:

Socialists believe that the continuing denial of our common humanity does not derive solely, or even primarily, from the sinful conduct of individuals but is institutionalised in the structures of economic, industrial, and political power which Christian churches may support, sustain, and even bless, while turning a blind eye to the injustices that continue unchecked. Socialists argue that neighbourly love must be sought in this world and not postponed until the next one.

Many Christian socialists like Benn believe capitalism to be idolatrous and rooted in the sin of greed. They identify the cause of inequality as the greed that they associate with capitalism – whereas Thatcher disassociated the two. As she crossed the threshold of 10 Downing Street on being elected in 1979, Thatcher recited a prayer which she wrongly attributed to St. Francis of Assisi:

> *Where there is discord, may we bring harmony. Where there is error, may we bring truth. Where there is doubt, may we bring faith. And where there is despair, may we bring hope.*

There has been speculation ever since about whether this was intended by Thatcher as a religious or a secular invocation, addressed to those doubting Thomases who had not yet been converted to the faith of Thatcherism.

In the 1980s, the Labour Party elected atheist leaders such as Michael Foot and Neil Kinnock, but they were followed by kirk-going John Smith, Anglo-Catholic Tony Blair, and son of the manse Gordon Brown. Blair once, somewhat simplistically, opined that "the Left got into trouble when its basic values became divorced from ....ethical socialism and Christian socialism".

Blair described his beliefs in a very personal, almost Biblical, way:

> *Socialism to me was never about nationalisation or the power of the state. It is a moral purpose to life, a set of values, a belief in society, in co-operation. It is how I try to live my life; the simple truths. I am worth no more than any other man, I am my brother's keeper, I will not walk by on the other side. We aren't simply people set in isolation from each other, face to face with eternity, but members of the same family, the community, the same human race.*

It was in stark contrast to the individualism of Thatcher, who famously stated that "there is no such thing as society....and no government can do anything except through people, and people must look after themselves first". Mrs Thatcher's obsession with wealth creation and thrift often distorted the message of Jesus:

> *No-one would remember the Good Samaritan if he had only good intentions; he had money as well.*

She interpreted the parable as teaching the necessity of having money and the charitable virtue of giving it to others: "For every Pharisee our [free-market] system produces, you will find at least three Good Samaritans". It was a charitable trickle-down effect which matched her faith in the economic trickle-down effect. Yet, is it likely that the priest and the Levite who walked by had no money? And, even if they were penniless, why did they completely ignore a beaten and stripped-naked man? The parable was about the power of love and compassion; not the power of money.

In spite of their religious views, both Thatcher and Blair were mesmerised by personal wealth and the power that accompanied it. Was it not Blair's temporal guru, Peter Mandelson (later Lord Mandelson), who was "intensely relaxed about people getting filthy rich"? Even fat cats could pass through the eye of a needle.

Although the Anglican Church was traditionally regarded as "the Tory party at prayer", fault lines appeared as that party moved from one-nation conservatism into full-throttled economic liberalism. In 1984, the Archbishop of Canterbury, Robert Runcie, set up a special commission to examine the strengths, insights, problems, and needs of the Anglican Church's life and mission in Urban Priority Areas. Its catalyst was the Toxteth riots in Liverpool three years before. The Commission's purpose was to reflect on the challenge that God might be making to church and nation at a time when the level of unemployment exceeded three million. Its basic belief, set out in its report, *Faith in the City*, was as follows;

> *The true nature of human life is to be discerned in the life of Jesus Christ ...we need to create a society in which benefits and burdens are shared in a more equitable way.*

Conservative politicians dismissed the report, before it was even published, as "pure Marxist theology", claiming that it proved that the Anglican Church was governed by a "load of Communist clerics". This claim was rather strange, since the Commission's chairman, Sir Richard O'Brien, was an unlikely Marxist, was a big wig of the Confederation of British Industry. Margaret Thatcher complained: "There's nothing about self-help or doing anything for yourself in the report" and she lamented its focus on state action.

Jesus, of course, had no view on wealth creation, or thrift, or whether the state should be large or small. His teachings centred on love for one's fellow beings and personal salvation. He did not teach what sort of society could best serve wealth creation and fairer wealth distribution.

There is individual Christian personal practice through charitable giving, and also collective state action when the market fails. The first is based on personal religious conviction, but the latter is, I think, based more on ethics. The socialist political theorist, Sir Bernard Crick, reminded us that "politics is ethics done in public".

The question is not whether the Church of England is still the Tory Party at prayer but whether it is Christianity in action. Perhaps this was in the mind of a Bishop of Winchester when he told his flock "to consider which manifesto comes nearest to what is morally right and just and never to be blindly loyal to a party you have always voted for in the past".

The electoral successes of both Thatcher and Blair were unlikely to be the result of convincing voters of the veracity of their personal religious beliefs. But they might have provided a certainty of political purpose and leadership which attracted voters.

Perhaps it is then ethics and morality, more than religion, which is more important to the conduct of politics. Indeed, the philosopher Mary Warnock in her book *Dishonest to God* stresses the need to prise religion apart from public morality and therefore separate it from politics and the law (see chapter 5). So, it is fruitless to ask whether Jesus was a bearded leftie. He was a radical, of course, with Messianic followers, but so was Margaret Thatcher and Jeremy Corbyn, who wears a beard but not a loin cloth.

The litmus test for public morality is not necessarily party dogma but whether governments attempt to understand the consequences of their actions and, most important, address and redress their unintended consequences. Such actions include supporting those who suffered under austerity, building more social housing to replace those sold off, providing adequate employment and support for the mining communities that they destroyed, and stabilising and rebuilding the countries that they bombed.

Morality is not about slavishly following political dogma or religious creeds. It is being able to step into other people's shoes. It is not just about voting for the party that will do best for you and your family. It is about supporting what is best for the nation as a whole; with particular concern for the needs of people who were of greatest concern to Jesus: the powerless and dispossessed. That requires not just spiritual empathy but a leap in political imagination.

Sources cited in this chapter

Archbishop of Canterbury's Commission on Urban Priority Areas. *Faith in the City – A Call for Action by Church and Nation.* 1985.

James G. Crossley. *Harnessing Chaos: The Bible in English Political Discourse Since 1968,* pp 20–26. Bloomsbury, 2014.

Eliza Filby. *The Battle for Britain's Soul: God and Mrs Thatcher.* Biteback Publishing, 2015.

Quintin Hogg. *The Case for Conservatism.* Penguin Books, 1947.

John Stuart Mill. *On Liberty, Utilitarianism and Other Essays.* Oxford World Classics, 2015.

R. H. Tawney. *Religion and the Rise of Capitalism.* Routledge, 1998.

Margaret Thatcher. *Speech to the General Assembly of the Church of Scotland.* Margaret Thatcher Foundation, 1988.

Mary Warnock. *Dishonest to God: On Keeping Religion out of Politics.* Continuum, 2010.

Rowan Williams. *On Christian Theology.* Blackwell, 2000.

7 Reverence for Life

The ethics of reverence for life is nothing but Jesus' great commandment to love – a commandment that is reached by thinking; religion and thinking meet in the mysticism of belonging to God through love.
(Albert Schweitzer)

When I was a boy attending Sunday school, I was enraptured by the teacher's reading of the life of a heroic figure. He was a missionary with a droopy moustache who wore a pith helmet as he played Bach on a battered piano in the middle of an African jungle. He also healed sick Africans. As children, of course, we were unaware of the moral concept of *reverence for life* that underpinned his life. We were more interested to know that Dr Schweitzer had a pet pelican. Yet *reverence for life* is at the heart of many controversial ethical issues argued about today – abortion, euthanasia, capital punishment, animal rights, nuclear testing, and the future of our planet and its eco-systems.

Most Unitarians believe that we humans hold the stewardship of our world in our hands and have an ethical responsibility for sustaining all life on this earth for future generations. After all, we humans are just one out of a world of some 8.4 million species, the majority of which have not yet even been identified. Indeed, some of these will become extinct even before they can be identified. For humanity to survive, it must learn to revere every form of life on earth. There is a strong ethical mysticism underlying *reverence for life.*

Although Schweitzer popularised it in the early twentieth century, *reverence for life* is an age-old philosophy, which possibly has its roots in Buddhism. One of the Buddha's precepts was to abstain from causing harm and taking life (both human and non-human). In the words of the Vietnamese Buddhist teacher, Thich Nhat Hanh:

For our practice to be deep and true, we must include the ecosystem..... The Diamond Sutra teaches us that it is impossible to distinguish between sentient and non-sentient beings. This is one of many ancient

> *Buddhist texts that teach deep ecology...... The practice of the First Precept is a celebration of reverence for life.*

This concept is also one of the five vows of the ancient Indian religion of Jainism, which Schweitzer had absorbed. The Jain mystic, Mahavir, born in the sixth century BCE, summed up this Ahimsa philosophy:

> *All life is bound together by mutual support and independence. One who neglects or disregards the existence of earth, air, water and vegetation disregards [sic] his own existence which is entwined with them.*

It extols non-violence and non-injury to all living things, not only in actions but in speech and thought. Whereas most people in the tropics would wear a mosquito veil to protect themselves from insects, Jain monks wear them to protect insects from humans.

By contrast, many influential theologians such as Saint Augustine did not interpret the Old Testament prohibition against killing as including animals; they are seen as dissociated from humans by their want of reason. This outlook centres on a hierarchical view of creation. Again, Saint Aquinas viewed creation as being created solely for humans and taught that the Divine Ordinance of animals and plants is preserved not for themselves but for humans. This is based on the belief that God revealed himself to the world as a human, not as an ape or ant. Both the life and death of animals are subject to our use; in other words, our exploitation. This instrumentalist understanding of non-human life was perpetuated by the Reformers, John Calvin and Martin Luther. In the words of Luther, "animals are subjected to man as to a tyrant who has absolute power over life and death", and this "gift" to humans shows how God is "favourably inclined to and friendly towards man".

Even though Albert Schweitzer was a Lutheran, he did not share Luther's concept of a human-centred universe:

> *We like to imagine that Man is nature's goal; but when we consider the immensity of the universe, we must confess that man is insignificant.*

Nor did he share Luther's view of a moral hierarchy which placed humanity at the apex of a pyramid of descending worth. The relationship between humanity and the animal world is an important part of *reverence for life*. Schweitzer had a purist view on what it should be:

> *When I injure any kind of life, I must be quite certain that it is necessary. I must never go beyond the unavoidable, not even in apparently insignificant things. The farmer who has mowed down a thousand flowers in his meadow in order to feed his cattle must be careful on his way home not to strike the head off a single flower by the side of the road in idle amusement, for he infringes on the law of life without being under the pressure of necessity.*

At his confirmation, young Albert was plagued with questions about how the Bible could be literally true. He could not accept in his heart his pastor's assurances that these things must simply be accepted as a matter of faith. Schweitzer wrote:

> *I was convinced — and I am so still — that the fundamental principles of Christianity have to be proved true by reasoning, and by no other method. Reason, I said to myself, has been given us that we may bring everything within the range of its action, even the most exalted ideas of religion.*

How very Unitarian! From the days of his Confirmation classes in Germany, he was unhappy with the tendency of many Christians to evade the issues of the ethical application of the teachings of Jesus:

> *As I looked about me, I realized only a few small sects, like the Unitarians and the Quakers, were the only real hope—they and the new modern spirit of humanism which might rekindle the true spirit of Jesus.*

Indeed, a Unitarian Universalist minister, the Revd Dr George Marshall, raised money for Schweitzer's missionary hospital and began to visit him in Lambarene, Gabon. By the end of the Second World War, it was only a

$4,300 gift from the Unitarian Service Committee that kept the hospital from having to close its doors for good. In due course, the minister invited Schweitzer to join his Church of the Larger Fellowship, and the great man accepted. But Schweitzer made it clear that he was not breaking his relationship with the Lutheran Church: he could remain on good terms with more than one religion.

Schweitzer believed that ethical values which could underpin the ideal of true civilisation had to have their foundation in deep thought and be world- and life-affirming. He therefore embarked on a search for ethical values in the various major religions and world views accessible to him. But he could not find any that were able, unequivocally, to combine ethics with life-affirmation. It was not until two years after moving out to Gabon that he finally found the simple statement which answered his quest.

In his autobiography *Out of My Life and Thought*, he explains this process. Having described how at the beginning of the summer of 1915 he awoke from some kind of mental daze, he asked himself why he was only criticising civilisation and not working on something constructive. He asked himself the question "what is civilisation?". His answer is illuminating:

> *The will to civilization is the universal will to progress that is conscious of the ethical as the highest value. In spite of the great importance we attach to the achievements of science and human prowess, it is obvious that only a humanity that is striving for ethical ends can benefit in full measure from material progress and can overcome the dangers that accompany it.*

He felt that the only possible way out of chaos is for us to adopt a concept of the world based on the ideal of true civilisation. For months on end, he lived in a continual state of mental agitation. Without the least success, he concentrated – even during his daily work at the hospital – on the real nature of the affirmation of life and of ethics and on the question of what they have in common. In his words, he was "wandering about in a thicket where no path was to be found and pushing against an iron door that would not yield". He then experienced an epiphany:

> *In that mental state I had to take a long journey up the river .... Lost in thought I sat on the deck of the barge, struggling to find the elementary and universal concept of the ethical that I had not discovered in any philosophy. I covered sheet after sheet with disconnected sentences merely to concentrate on the problem. Two days passed. Late on the third day, at the very moment when, at sunset, we were making our way through a herd of hippopotamuses, there flashed upon my mind, unforeseen and unsought, the phrase: "Ehrfurcht vor dem Leben" ("reverence for life"). The iron door had yielded. The path in the thicket had become visible.*

But is there not a dilemma here for a physician of the body who is also a physician of the soul? A doctor's *raison d'être* is to prevent disease. The moral dilemma is whether or not to kill insects which have cost the lives of millions of Africans through malaria. Even today as many as 850,000 Africans die through malaria – mostly young children. Perhaps the ethical test is whether the killing or sacrifice has a moral purpose. In her seminal work *Silent Spring*, which was dedicated to Schweitzer, the ecologist, Rachel Carson, exposed the use of the insecticide DDT. It was a scorched-earth policy which began poisoning the eco-system. Its use was the very negation of *reverence for life*. Many years later, the Chinese scientist, Tu YouYou, discovered a natural antidote to malaria – artemisinin. It has saved millions of human lives; not through killing insects but by treating humans.

Schweitzer's community action was founded on his premise that human beings are truly ethical when they obey the compulsion to assist all life and shrink from injuring anything that lives. It goes beyond humanism. It is not human-centric but life-centric. This compulsion derives from a deep awareness of, and sensitivity to, the prevalence of suffering; whether it affects one of his patients or his pet pelican.

> *Only in rare moments have I felt really glad to be alive. I cannot help but feel the suffering all around me, not only of humanity but the whole of creation. I have never tried to withdraw myself from the community of suffering. It seemed to me a matter of course that we should take our share of the burden of pain that lies upon the world. When seeing*

> *suffering we must be challenged by a desire for redemption, to help all creatures. There is always mystery. The mystery of pain. And we come to be always conscious of our great responsibility to alleviate it.*

This feeling was illumined by a poignant event that Schweitzer experienced. It is perhaps a modern version of the parable of the Good Samaritan:

> *I saw a man lying on the ground with his head almost buried in the sand and ants running all over him. He was a victim of sleeping sickness. His companions had left him there, probably some days before, because they could take him no further. He was past all help, though he still breathed. While I was busied with him, I could see through the door of the hut the bright blue waters of the bay in their frame of green woods, a scene of magic beauty, looking still more enchanting in the flood of golden light poured over by the setting sun. To be shown in a single glance such a paradise and such helpless, hopeless misery was overwhelming.*

Albert Schweitzer died in 1965 at the age of 90. He was buried in his hospital's grounds just off the shores of the River Ogowe. In his coffin were placed his battered pith helmet and a bag of rice that he used to carry to feed his animals. The river is not just a river but a river system, three or four branches twisting together. Like that river, the quest for Schweitzer's *reverence for life* winds and snakes, reaching forwards and backwards in fits and starts. That river continues to flow for those who have the courage to navigate that difficult journey.

So, was Schweitzer a saint? He was a follower of Christ, but perhaps, more a metaphysical agnostic who saw religion primarily in terms of ethics. The theologian Don Cupitt describes him as "a tragic Christian, a man of iron will and determination.... the tragic Christian has to be strong". He needed to be strong in order to endure the arduous physical and spiritual journey that he had set for himself.

Sources cited in this chapter

Ara Paul Barsam. *Reverence for Life: Albert Schweitzer's Great Contribution to Ethical Thought*. Oxford University Press, 2008.

Rachel Carson. *Silent Spring*. Penguin Books, 2000.

Albert Schweitzer. *Out of My Life and Thought*. John Hopkins University Press, 1998.

Thich Nhat Hanh. *The Diamond That Cuts Through Illusion: Commentaries on the Prajnaparamita Diamond Sutra*. Parallax Press, 2010.

8 From Marxism to Mysticism

> *It is necessary to uproot yourself. Cut down the tree and make a cross and carry it forever after.*
> (Simone Weil)

As the Unitarian Universalist Revd Tom Owen-Towle has stated "rationalism without a sense of mystery grows sterile and mysticism untempered by reason falls prey to credulity". To many of us, mystics throughout the ages seem like aesthetes living a singular life; closeted in a separate, ethereal world. Yet, rather than being equanimous, Christian mysticism can be rooted in reality and quite challenging. This sentiment is expressed by Unitarian Universalist mystic, Revd Jacob Trapp:

> *I like to think of mysticism as the art of meeting reality, the art of richer and deeper awareness. It is an experience that comes unbidden... it is not the intellectual conviction that Being is my being, but rather an ineffable experience of the Oneness, flooding in to overwhelm our illusion of loneliness, separateness.*

The concept of a supernatural, external deity is seen as a violation of the oneness of the universe. The fourteenth-century Christian, Meister Eckhart, believed that between a person and God there is no distinction: "the same eye with which I look at God is the eye with which God looks at me". John Shelby Spong, the retired bishop of Newark, New Jersey, thinks that when mystics like Eckhart talk about God, they appear to be talking about an unbounded presence unfettered by creeds, doctrines, and dogmas. It is a timeless reality which the theologian Paul Tillich called "the Eternal Now". Spong experiences God as "expanded consciousness"; when we evolve from a "being of survival" to a "being of love".

This love is pure and unconditional. Emanating from a deep love of fellow human beings in the oneness of our universe, it leads naturally to liberal social action. It is a pool of love not polluted by the promise of the reward of heaven or the threat of hell. In the words of the Buddha:

> *If there is no other world and there is no fruit and ripening of actions well done or ill done, then here and now in this life I shall be freed from hostility, affliction and anxiety and I shall live happily.*

The African-American Baptist and civil-rights activist the Revd Howard Thurman argues for “affirmative mysticism”. He sees God moving through our social structures as well as through our personal experience, inspiring the spiritual and interpersonal unity of all things. Going beyond self-interest to world loyalty, the mystic sees our common humanity and empathises with the suffering of the oppressed. Mystics embrace contrasting viewpoints, even viewpoints that they continue to oppose, as ways of moving from polarisation to reconciliation. Accordingly, when the mystic observes conditions that threaten a person’s encounter with God, he or she is compelled to confront them. In the words of Thurman:

> *Social action, therefore, is an expression of resistance against whatever tends to, or separates one from, the experience of God, who is the ground of his being.....It has to do with the removal of all that prevents God from coming to himself in the life of the individual. Whatever there is that blocks this, calls for action.*

One can gain the world, as Jesus says, and lose one’s soul, caught up in consumerism, power, entitlement, and self-gratification. In the immortal words of William Wordsworth:

> *The world is too much with us; late and soon,*
> *Getting and spending, we lay waste our powers;*
> *Little we see in Nature that is ours;*
> *We have given our hearts away, a sordid boon!*

Thurman believes that the oppressor’s injustice ultimately stunts her or his own soul, as well as the souls of those whom they oppress. Inspired by a sense of the unity and divinity of all life, the mystic seeks the healing of both oppressor and oppressed.

Self-denial and altruism are also integral qualities of the mystic. It is expressed in the uncomfortable and uncompromising words of the poet and Soviet dissident Anna Akhmatova:

Don't torment your heart with earthly joys
Don't cling to your wife (sic) or your home,
Take the bread from your child
To give it to a stranger.
And be the humblest servant of the one
Who was your bitterest foe,
And call the beast of the forest brother,
And don't ask God for anything, ever.

Someone whose life exemplified self-sacrifice and social action was the twentieth-century French mystic, Simone Weil. She was no chaise- longue mystic waiting for a heavenly vision. She was a woman of action, someone who embarked on a fascinating journey in her too short life: from becoming a Jewish atheist with Marxist leanings to becoming a mystical Christian holding very anti-collectivist beliefs. In the early part of this journey, she was known as the "Red Virgin", but towards the end of her life became more a "Bride of Christ".

Weil was born in 1909 in Paris, the child of a prosperous doctor and his wife. She was a brilliant student and passed the entrance exams for the elite Ecole Normale Supérieure, beating her namesake, Simone De Beauvoir, into second place. Yet she always questioned her own intellectual ability. At the age of fifteen she experienced months of inward darkness, until she discovered the importance of *attention* – a realisation that the realm of truth is open to everyone.

Throughout her life she had a powerful empathy with the suffering of others. Even at the age of five at the outbreak of the First World War, she refused to eat sugar since it was not available to the French soldiers. As an adult, she refused to have heating in her rooms because such comfort was not available to the unemployed.

Her first job was that of a philosophy teacher at a girls' *lycée,* at which time she led a demonstration of the unemployed before the city council.

It caused an enormous uproar – a conservative newspaper branding her as a "red virgin of the tribe of Levi, bearer of Muscovite gospels". This was a gross distortion. She probably was a virgin and was certainly of the Jewish race, but she certainly was not a political ideologue taking orders from Moscow. Indeed, although she admired revolutionaries like Trotsky for advancing the struggle of the working class for economic power, she did not share their narrow materialistic and deterministic ideology. There had to be roses, not just bread, in any revolution. When the exiled Trotsky spent a few days as a guest in the Weil household in 1933, the 24-year-old bent his ear about the tyranny of the Soviet state over the Russian people. He, however, resolutely defended comrade Stalin; it was a pity she did not warn him of his impending assassination by a Stalinist ice pick.

Weil took a sabbatical and, with a strong impulse to become "a slave of capital", she began to do manual jobs in factories. She wanted to experience the chronic state of the factory workers "which grips them through the senses, their bodies, the thousand and one little details that crowd the minutes of which their lives are constituted". A romantic idealist, she conceives of an ideal factory that could fill the soul through powerful awareness of the collective life –where the worker feels indispensable, not insignificant. Weil was thus a political activist, practising what she preached ("Which factory did Marx ever work in?", she asked). She turned Descartes' statement on its head. She replaced "I think, therefore I am" with "I will, therefore I am".

An important event that changed her views was the Spanish Civil War. She had initially been a pacifist, but she recognised that violence – provided it was used in a controlled way – could be morally right in order to prevent fascism from crushing the soul and extinguishing human dignity. So, in 1936 she joined the Republican Front. She was associated with an international group allied with an anarchist trade union in Aragon. But a few weeks later – a touch of bathos here – she stepped into a pot of boiling oil and had to be invalided home. She had by this time become disillusioned with the struggle, which she felt had forgotten the objective of alleviating the plight of the poor.

She then reverted to pacifism, believing that force corrupts those who use it and those who suffer from it. In 1942, the family escaped from

Vichy France to New York. She did, however, want to join the resistance movement quartered in London. Her proposal was to parachute a nursing squad to the Front Line in the hope that she and others could be at the side of France's soldiers as they fought the Nazis troops. It was yet another example of Weil's idealism, but it was regarded as an impractical piece of romantic whimsy and rejected by Charles de Gaulle.

Throughout her life, Weil dressed in flat shoes, a beret, and dour tweedy suits. She wore no makeup – a mystic without lipstick. She was seen by fellow students as a walking brain – a Mekon – a purely intellectual being. Her personal life was inextricably linked to her thinking. Sexual purity to her was as instinctive as breathing, and any form of sentimentality in life was scarcely necessary. She came from a happy family background. But in her quest for the deepest truth, which for her had an impersonal quality, she felt that personal intimacy would lead down a blind alley in respect to the perfection of God. A relative once kissed the five-year-old Simone's hand. But she drew it away in horror and scrubbed it vigorously with carbolic soap. Was this just an instinct for excessive cleanliness or the first sign of her quest for spiritual perfection?

Weil always stated that she never sought God. God came to her as she waited – and God came through Christianity. She had come from an atheist Jewish family. Although she had never even visited a synagogue, she was, of course, classed as a Jew in Vichy France and as such she was deprived of her profession as a teacher. She vehemently objected to this; not necessarily because it was anti-Semitic, but because she had never been a practising Jew.

The shrillness of her denunciation of Judaism during that age of rampant anti-Semitism is rather disconcerting. Christianity has historically had a strong built-in resistance to recognising the religious reality and validity of Judaism. In France, it had resulted in the expulsion of Jews in the thirteenth and fourteenth centuries. In Weil's time, the Vichy government collaborated with the Nazis in deporting thousands of French Jews to the death camps. Weil had, however, the blinkered view that there are two kinds of religion: good and evil. The good religion is that of Christian-based mysticism, while Judaism is the archetype of a bad religion, based on nationalism and the use of force.

Yet Weil never entered the Roman Catholic Church. She was never baptised, so was not able to take the sacraments. She clung always to her sense of being an outsider among the religious. She did not want to be exposed to what she called "the patriotism of the Church". She even believed that God did not want her to enter the Church. In her words, she was an "apostle to the Gentiles", planted at the "intersection of Christianity and everything that is not Christianity". She wrote to her confidant and friend, the Dominican, Father Perrin:

> *I have never once had, even for a moment, the feeling that God wants me to be in the Church. Unless I'm mistaken, I should stay outside for the future too, except perhaps at the moment of death.*

She thought that formally entering the Church would result in the pain of separating herself from the immense and unfortunate multitude of unbelievers. In fact, she believed that the unbelief of many atheists is closer to a true love of God and a true sense of his nature than the kind of easy faith that has never been rooted in a mystical experience of God. The paradox was that it is easier for a non-Christian to become a true Christian than it is for a religious Christian to become one. Weil believed that the implicit love of God can have objectives here below in which God is really secretly present. One of these is the love of one's neighbour which, of course, is very much part of the essence of Christianity.

Weil states that she entered Christianity through mystical experiences. She felt that Christ had taken possession of her, as she left her flesh huddled in the corner of a monastery. God can cross the universe and come to us:

> *Over the infinity of space and time, the infinitely more infinite love of God comes to possess us. He comes at his own time. We have the power to consent to receive him or to refuse. If we remain deaf, he comes back again and again like a beggar, but also like a beggar, one day he stops coming.*

She saw God as removed from the world, but believed that humans could contact God. It was rather like a prisoner separated by a wall from another prisoner whom he cannot see. But he is able to communicate with him through tapping out very basic messages on the pipe connecting the two cells.

Weil states that if we consent, then God "puts a little seed in us and he goes away again". All we have to do is wait. The seed grows itself, but the process is painful and we cannot avoid destroying what ever gets in its way. But then:

> *A day comes when the soul belongs to God, when it not only consents to love but when truly and effectively it loves. Then, in turn it must cross the universe to go to God.*

Weil seemed always in danger of becoming a slave to her own immense intellect; a lonely moral scourge whose magnificent capacity to dream of what ought to be was somehow imprisoned by her own pessimism of the turbulent world at that time. As a purist intellectual, she sustained all possible beliefs in their contradictions of the shallow materialism of radical politics, the coldness of atheism, and the smug complacency and hypocrisy of the Church. From each, she tried to seek its partial truth, and in doing never achieved the whole truth she craved for. Yet the wondrousness of her short life was her personal sacrifice to social action, which underpinned her spiritual journey even to its end. On arriving in England to help the war effort, she became ill. In April 1943, she was diagnosed with tuberculosis. She could have survived, but she ate only morsels of food, on the grounds that she wanted to eat no more than the meagre fare that ordinary French people under Nazi occupation were eating. She even had to be force-fed in the hospital. Weil died at the age of 34 and was buried in Ashford, Kent, mourned by just a handful of London friends. Inscribed on her gravestone are the words: "My solitude held in its grasp the grief of others until my death". As God's companion, she had sacrificed her life in promoting God's vision "on earth as it is in heaven".

Sources cited in this chapter

Richard Boeke. *Mysticism and Social Action: Lawrence Lecture and Discussions with Dr Howard Thurman*. International Association for Religious Freedom, 2014.

Robert Coles. *Simone Weil: A Modern Pilgrimage*, Addison-Wesley, 1989.

Tom Owen-Towle. Freethinking *Mystics with Hands: Exploring the Heart of Unitarian Universalism*. Skinner House Books. 1998.

Howard Thurman. *The Inward Journey*. Friends United Press, 2007.

Jacob Trapp. *Return to the Springs*. Skinner House Books. 1987.

Simone Weil. *Waiting for God* . Harper & Row, 1973.

9 Satyagraha: The Force for Truth and Love

In the mist of death, life persists; in the midst of untruth, truth persists; in the midst of darkness, light persists. Hence, I gather that God is Life, Truth and Love. He is the supreme God.
(Mahatma Gandhi)

Some time ago, a Unitarian minister friend took me to the London Coliseum to see Philip Glass's opera, *Satyagraha*. The libretto was taken from the epic Hindu scriptural poem, the *Bhagavad Gita*. Consisting of seven hundred stanzas written between the fifth and second centuries BCE, it presents a somewhat protracted conversation between Krishna and Arjuna. The minimalist music was typical of Glass, and it was sung in the original Sanskrit. I was, however, mesmerised by the opera, and it reawakened my interest in Gandhi, who had used the term "Satyagraha" to capture his concept of non-violent resistance to injustice.

Ironically, Gandhi, a devout Hindu, was only introduced to the *Gita* by two Englishmen when he was studying for the Bar in London. It was to become his "infallible guide of conduct ... a dictionary of daily reference". Interpreting the texts literally, orthodox Hindus regarded the *Gita* as the historical account of a battle in which one martial leader sought to avoid bloodshed but was soon reminded by God of his caste obligation to commit violence. The *Gita* states that, since it is only the body that dies and not the soul, why not kill when it is your soldierly duty to do so? Gandhi, however, always wanted to interrogate the scriptures until they gave answers that he felt were applicable to him: they had to be authentic. He sees the *Gita* as using the guise of physical warfare to describe the duel that perpetually goes on in the hearts of mankind. The apostle of non-violence, he thus felt free to propound a different interpretation. Since we are all parts of God who is perfect, how can we and why should we kill?

This belief was the basis of Satyagraha. The word "Satya" (Truth) is derived from "Sat" (Being). Gandhi believed that nothing is or exists in reality except truth. Where there is truth, there is knowledge; and where there is no knowledge, there can be no truth. He believed that truth is the sole justification for our existence, and all our activities must be centred on it. This requires single-minded devotion to the truth, and indifference to all other interests in life. One person's truth might not, however, be that of another person. God himself appears to different individuals in different aspects. So, there is nothing wrong in each person following truth according to his or her lights – and indeed it is their duty to do so. Even if a devotee stumbles on the wrong path in the selfless search for truth, he or she will be redirected to the right path.

Of all the moral principles, for Gandhi truth was the first and foremost. He called it "the sovereign principle". It implied truthfulness not merely in speech, but in thought also; "and not only the relative truth of our conception, but the absolute truth, the eternal principle, that is God". He thus equated God with truth:

> *I worship God as truth only. I have not yet found him, but I am seeking after him. I am prepared to sacrifice the things dearest to me in pursuit of this quest.... Often in my progress, I have had faint glimpses of the absolute truth, God, and daily the conviction is growing upon me that the above is real and all else is unreal.*

Much is known of the life's work of the great man, Mahatma Gandhi. His successful efforts to free India from British control. His vain attempts to unify India – Hindus and Moslems. His championing of the rights of the dispossessed: the so-called Untouchables, child brides in India and indentured Asian serfs in South Africa. His opposition to unjust taxes such as the Salt Tax, and imports of cotton goods which impoverished the Indian people. All this was achieved through passive resistance or non-co-operation, *Satyagraha*. He relied not on force but on love for those who violently resisted his demands and who would imprison him and murder his followers.

Gandhi's actions were political, but his beliefs were spiritual:

> *Men say that I am a saint losing myself in politics. The fact is I am a politician trying my hardest to be a saint.*

His religion made him political. His politics were religious. Gandhi followed Yogic ideals required by the devotee, as set out in the *Gita*:

> *The devotee who is jealous of none, who is a fount of all mercy, who is without egotism, who is selfless, who treats alike cold and heat, happiness and misery, who is ever forgiving, who is always contented, whose resolutions are firm, who has a dedicated mind and soul to God, ... who renounces all fruit, good or bad, who treats friend and foe alike ..... Such devotion is inconsistent with the existence at the same time of strong attachments.*

Gandhi summarised all these attributes, including the absence of attachments, in one word: "desirelessness". These thoughts are not confined to Hinduism. Gandhi saw similarities in Jesus's teaching in the Sermon on the Mount:

> *Whosoever shall smite thee on thy right cheek, turn to him the other also. And if any man take away thy coat, let him have thy cloak too ... Blessed are ye, when men revile you ... Love your enemies, bless them that curse you. Lay not up for treasures upon earth. For where your treasure is, there will your heart be also.*

Desirelessness manifested itself in "*Brahmacharya*", which signifies control of all the senses at all times and in all places in thought, word, and deed. It includes yet transcends dietary restraint; the Mahatma was a lifelong vegetarian. It also involves sexual restraint. At the age of thirteen, Gandhi had married his fourteen-year-old wife and was celibate from the age of 37 to his death at 77. Although he lived in marital chastity, he actually slept alongside two young women, explaining it as an experiment to test his abstinence. The obvious question one has to ask, however, is why could he not do this by sleeping next to his wife? He was an aesthete who eschewed close attachment; perhaps with a sense of shame about his previous sexual contact as a husband. The spiritual father of his nation felt he had to abandon his duties as a husband and father of his children.

Brahmacharya rules out hate, anger, violence, and untruth. It creates equability. Perfect Brachmacharis, Gandhi wrote, are "perfectly sinless". They are therefore near to God. They are like God. It was this ultimate state of self-transformation that he aspired to. He lived this way of life in the ashrams or communities that he established in South Africa and India. He was not, however, a remote, ascetic mystic, for his whole belief system centred on action, whether it was political campaigning or practical work, such as doing routine chores that usually the Untouchables would do, such as the cleaning of the ashram latrines. Social action was the essence of *Brahmacharya*, but only if it was done without wishing to taste its fruit.

Satyagraha was the political tool of the Brahmachari. If words fail to convince the adversary, perhaps purity, humility, and honesty will. The opponent must be weaned from error by patience and sympathy – weaned not crushed, converted not annihilated. It was the exact opposite of the Old Testament saying of an eye for an eye which would only result in making everyone blind.

The first test of *Satyagraha* was experienced when Gandhi moved from London to practise as a barrister in South Africa. It was in opposition to the compulsory registration and finger-printing of Asians in South Africa (The Black Act) in 1906 – not unlike the future pass laws in South Africa. It involved the mass burning of registration certificates and the imprisonment of Gandhi. The law reflected deep-rooted racialism. The Boer leader, General Jan Smuts, urged that "the Asiatic cancer which has already eaten so deeply into the vitals of South Africa ought to be eradicated". Many years later, Gandhi gave Smuts a pair of sandals which he had made in prison. On Gandhi's birthday, Smuts returned them as a gesture of friendship: "I have worn these sandals for many a summer, even though I feel I am not worthy to stand in the shoes of such a great man". This was the transformative power of Gandhi's love.

Satyagraha involved many other powerful symbols. One of the most dramatic and powerful symbolic gestures was the Salt March. In 1930, Gandhi organised opposition to the salt tax. He and 78 disciples walked two hundred miles from the ashram at Sabarmati to Dandi on the coast. Along the way peasants kneeled by the roadside as the pilgrims passed. On arriving, the Mahatma told his followers that he was about to "give a signal to the nation" – and he took a few crystals of salt from the shore. It was an illegal act: salt-tax evasion. This small act set off a chain of events that led to mass passive resistance to the tax, the brutal suppression of the protesters, and imprisonment of many, including Gandhi himself. The British had beaten the Indians with batons and rifle butts. The passive resisters neither cringed, nor complained, nor retreated. England had lost its moral authority to a few crystals of sea salt, had rendered itself powerless, and made the Indian people feel invincible.

After the Salt March, when Gandhi was negotiating with the Viceroy, Lord Irwin, he was offered a cup of tea. "Did he take sugar?" "No thank you", he replied, putting a pinch of salt into his tea. "This will remind me of our own Boston Tea Party at Dandi," he said. They both laughed. Winston Churchill was not, however, amused at "the nauseating and humiliating spectacle of this one-time Inner Temple lawyer, now seditious fakir, striding half naked up the steps of the Viceroy's palace, there to negotiate and to parley on equal terms with the representative of the King-Emperor". But Gandhi even took tea with King George V and Queen Mary at Buckingham Palace wearing his loin cloth. He was asked if he felt underdressed in the company of the King-Emperor. "Fortunately, his majesty was wearing enough clothes for both of us", he replied.

Another symbol of *Satyagraha* was spinning. Indians began to spin cotton for their own clothes – *khadi* – and publicly burned cotton goods from Lancashire that were impoverishing them. This economic boycott, known as "*Hartu*", was a challenge to the whole raison d' être of British imperialism, which was the creation of a market for British exports. One would have expected the Lancashire cotton workers to have deeply resented Gandhi. Yet when he visited Green Field Mill in Darwen, he was mobbed as a hero by the mill lasses.

Gandhi and his followers spun for at least an hour each day throughout their lives. It almost became a liturgical act. The spinning-wheel symbol is ever-present in India – even on its national flag. Even his name was a symbol. The poet Rabindranath Tagore gave him the name of "Mahatma", meaning "the great soul in beggar's garb". It was a dress code which he adopted in order to mourn comrades killed during the South African miners' strike which he led.

Satyagraha was also associated with fasting. Gandhi used to fast, but not as a form of moral blackmail. He did not believe that it should be used to further any cause that he would directly benefit from, such as hastening independence. He fasted almost to death in a bid to end the shunning and segregation of the Untouchables and to reverse three thousand years of inhumanity. If even the shadow of an Untouchable passed over a Brahmin, the latter would have to thoroughly cleanse himself. The Mahatma's last fast was aimed at uniting India: to prevent the religious riots and killings between Hindus, Moslems, and Sikhs before the partition of India. Although Gandhi was a devout Hindu, there was a strong humanist dimension to him:

> *Humanity is an ocean; if a few drops of the ocean are dirty, the ocean does not become impure....I know I cannot find God apart from humanity...I claim to know my millions. All the hours of the day I am with them. They are my first care and last because I recognise no God except that God that is to be found in the hearts of those millions.*

It was for them that he fasted: "I put my head on God's lap, and God sent me to fast." It was a process of self-purification; of mass self-purification. The Mahatma's weight fell to 107 lbs. After solemn pledges were made by leaders of the religious communities, Gandhi broke his fast with the Hindu prayer:

> *Lead me from untruth to truth*
> *From darkness to light*
> *From death to immortality.*

But even the Mahatma could not achieve the Herculean task of forging the religious and political unity of the sub-continent. In 1948 he was shot by a Hindu fanatic who perversely believed that his removal would lead to the violent reunification of India under Hindu dominance. Yet even the murderer bowed to him in reverence before pulling the trigger. The Mahatma's pyre burned for fourteen hours, during which the priests recited the *Gita*'s seven hundred verses.

Gandhi's legacy is not pacifism. *Satyagraha* is active, not passive. The Satyagrahis resist the enemy, but they will do it from the position of love:

> *We must widen the prison gates and we must enter them as a bridegroom enters the bride's chamber. Freedom is to be wooed only inside prison walls and sometimes on gallows, never in the council chamber or the court.*

His death was the ultimate sacrifice in the pursuit of freedom and truth through universal love of humanity. This is what independent India's first Prime Minister, Jawaharlal Nehru, said on hearing of his mentor's death:

> *The light has gone out of our lives and there is darkness everywhere ... Yet I am wrong ... for the light that shone in this country was no ordinary light ... For that light represented something more than the immediate present; it represented the living, the eternal truths, reminding us of the right path, drawing us from error, taking this ancient country to freedom.*

Sources cited in this chapter

Louis Fischer. *The Life of Mahatma Gandhi*. Granada, 1982.

Jack Hawley. *The Bhagavad Gita: A Walkthrough for Westerners*. New World Library, 2001.

10 A Communion for Humanity

We light the spark of God within ourselves when we serve others and bring a bit of glow and joy to other people's lives.
(Norbert Capek)

The taking of Communion is, of course, always associated with the liturgical tradition of the Last Supper. Jesus took bread, and when he had given thanks he broke it, saying; "This is my body which is broken for you. Do this in remembrance of me." In the same way he also took the cup after the supper, saying "This is the new covenant in my blood. Do this, as often as you drink it, in remembrance of me." These simple acts were powerful symbols to help the disciples remember him and, unknown to them, to prepare them for his imminent demise.

The Catholic Church had to adopt a more dramatic, literal interpretation. In 1551, the Council of Trent decreed that "by the consecration of the bread and wine there takes place a change of the whole substance of the bread into the substance of the body of Christ our Lord and of the whole substance of the wine into the substance of his blood". This is the doctrine of transubstantiation.

Participation in the act of Communion is, of course, still regularly observed by both Catholic and Anglican congregations today, as the sacrament of the Eucharist. There is, however, a difference between the faiths. Protestants simply celebrate Communion in memory of the Last Supper, recalling its symbolic importance in the life of Jesus.

For us Unitarians, Communion is more about communal sharing – from the Latin "communio". For some, the taking of bread and wine, like other liturgical rituals, forms a barrier rather than a ladder to God. In the words of the Canadian poet, Alden Nowlan:

The times I have tasted your flesh there was no bread and wine between us.... only night and the wind beating the grass.

That is why many Unitarian congregations have opted for an alternative. The *Flower Communion* was devised by the Unitarian minister, Norbert

Capek and his wife, Maja. He introduced it to his congregation in St Nicholas's Church, Prague in 1923. The tradition of the Flower Communion has its roots in Capek's ideal of harmony among people: living together in fellowship.. It is a powerful symbol of his religious humanism:

> *What kind of religion is this Unitarianism? It is humanity lightened by divinity. It is humanism and theism combined. It is not the kind of humanism without God and without a soul, but the humanism of those great individuals who from time to time called our nation to a new life...... What else is it but to begin with humankind when seeking God?*

Capek defines the theology of the Unitarian Church thus: God is both transcendent and immanent, and God is manifested in human practical activity. God works through people's understanding of their total responsibility and awareness of the necessity of their practical deeds for the development and improvement of themselves and their world. In other words, what is important are deeds not creeds.

Capek believed that it is necessary for each individual to be fully responsible for his or her life, instead of wasting time searching for an external determining authority. One must consider one's own situation in order to learn how to live a healthy life in both religious and psychological terms. Also, one needs to consider the broader situation of humanity with a view towards the continuous improvement of society's living conditions through social change. People are responsible for their environment, and even for the whole of creation and nature. This thinking was not unlike Albert Schweitzer's "reverence for life" (see Chapter 7). Capek's theology links Christianity with humanity; the human attributes of Christ are more sacred than any metaphysical properties he might have:

> *How many people doth find the heart of religion in certain mysteries woven round the birth and death of Christ? Yet I see it in the way Christ took a child in his arms. How he grasped the hand of a lost sinner. The heart of a church doth reveal the personal qualities of its members that manifest themselves in all that they do.*

The main purpose of the Flower Communion is to sustain this theology. Each congregant brings a flower to be used in the service; congregants leave their flowers in a central location, either as they enter or during the service. Early in the service the bouquets of flowers are brought forward, often by children. Towards the end of the service, the flowers are distributed, or congregants come forward and choose a flower different from the one they brought. Capek explains the ritual's symbolism;

> *We have chosen flowers, nature's most tender, common and beautiful gift, as our symbol and sacrament. Each of us is symbolised in a flower. Flowers in a vase symbolise fellowship, our commonality. The way we brought and carried away the flowers symbolises voluntarism, freedom. When you leave this meeting in peace and without rush, each of you take a blossom out of the bouquet of blooms without being able to choose who you want to accept as brother and sister.*

So, the Flower Communion represents an unconditional unity: a spiritual unity. It symbolises an uncompromised equality of people. It is about celebrating racial, religious, and cultural diversity – the very antithesis of the uniformity of totalitarianism.

Our Flower Communion is a modest celebration in which we are not subjected to any magic, mysterious, or supernatural powers or beings. No bells or spells; just smells. Instead, it symbolises human mutual understanding, empathy, sharing, and forgiveness. It symbolises the commonality of faith and life, not the conformity of belief.

The communion is not about giving a flower to one individual but giving to the congregation as a whole. The bouquet is more beautiful than the sum of the individual flowers that form it. The giving is not even about receiving love, forgiveness, or even thanks, for there is no-one to thank you for receiving your flower. No-one knows whose flower they have chosen; it could be someone you know well, or someone you know not at all. So, the giving is selfless and unconditional.

Indeed, giving can be about helping those who you don't know. That is the message of the parable of the Good Samaritan. Unlike the priest and Levite, he didn't pass by a man who had fallen among robbers who left him half dead:

When he saw him, he was moved with compassion,
came to him, and bound up his wounds, pouring on oil and wine. He
set him on his own animal, brought him to an inn,
and took care of him.

But giving is not just about practical help but about showing emotional connection to strangers. This is illustrated by a real-life story. A man wracked by depression began walking across the Golden Bridge in San Francisco. But he did not reach the other side. When his body was pulled out of the sea, an envelope was found in his pocket addressed to "whom it might concern":

If someone had looked into my eyes and smiled during my walk across the bridge, I would have kept on walking to the other side and started a new life. But no-one looked at me. No-one smiled.

It is a letter addressed to all of us. We live in a world with individuals either colliding or drifting apart. We need to look at people as though God has just looked at them. We must try to see his reflection in their eyes and let it touch our hearts and then smile on them. We need to establish loving communities based on mutual trust and common understanding, acting in a common purpose crossing nations, races, and faiths.

Capek's beliefs centred on the importance of this human connection:

Let us renew our resolution sincerely to be brothers and sisters
regardless of any kind of barriers which estrange person from person.
In this holy resolution may we be strengthened; knowing that we are
one family; one spirit, the spirit of love, unites us; and that our work
together for a more perfect and more joyful life leads us on.

His spiritual journey is symbolised by the beautiful blooms of his Flower Communion services in Prague, and by the twigs and stones that he used for his communion in Dachau just before he was murdered by the Nazis. He was born in Bohemia in 1870, which has been the cradle of liberal religion for centuries. Born into a very modest family, he was brought up as a Roman Catholic. Disillusioned with that Church's dogma, he became a Baptist at the age of eighteen and then a minister. Even early in his Baptist ministry he was seen to embody Unitarian values. In 1910, he had a long conversation with Professor Thomas Masaryk, who was later to become the founding President of an independent Czechoslovakia. After listening to his views and beliefs, the great liberal thinker and statesman identified him as more a Unitarian than a Baptist.

Preaching in the USA, Capek found his increasingly liberal views were at odds with the Baptist creed. He was even tried for heresy by a Baptist tribunal, but was eventually acquitted. It was in the USA where he was greatly influenced by Unitarianism. He began to attend the First Unitarian Church of Essex County, where he found "not only clear heads but warm hearts". On returning to his birth land, he set up the Prague Convention of Liberal Religious Fellowship in 1922 and eventually was ordained a Unitarian minister, as was his wife. In 1930, the Unitarian Church was officially recognised by the Czech government under President Masaryk.

Even though he was small in stature, Capek had a great intellectual presence. He was a very charismatic preacher and sometimes drew more than 3,000 people into his services. His church had the largest congregation of any Unitarian church in the world. Although he spent much time on pastoral duties, he wrote 90 hymns, some of them still sung today. He was also very much a family man; he and his wife raised eleven children.

After the Nazi invasion of his homeland (by then part of Czechoslovakia), Capek was invited to return to the safety of the USA. Instead, he courageously remained to continue preaching against tyranny, declaring the need for freedom to his congregation, which was often infiltrated by undercover Nazis. Like Gandhi, he believed in the sovereignty of truth:

> *The church's task must be to place truth above any tradition, spirit above any scripture, freedom above authority, and progress above all reaction.*

His sermons proclaiming the spiritual foundations of truth and democracy were seen as a danger to the repressive regime of the Third Reich, but this did not deter him.

I say to you that to be conquered and remain lying down is weakness. But to be conquered and to stand up is heroism.

Regarded by the Nazis as a turbulent priest, Capek was arrested by the Gestapo, imprisoned, and transported to Dachau, ostensibly for listening to foreign broadcasts. The privations were unbearable: inmates were so driven by hunger that they dug for earthworms for nourishment. Capek was beaten by the guards, but his love for his fellowmen could never be ground down:

Blow, angry winds, through my stony body. You will not conquer my soul. Whoever has broken his shackles and given wings to his mind is marching into a golden future.

He often saved his meagre slice of bread to share with his fellow prisoners in a communion service. Twigs and stones were substituted for flowers as part of the simple liturgy. Prisoners of all faiths and none participated and were strengthened by this symbol of communal love. Surviving fellow prisoners tell in glowing words of the magnificence of his witness to the truths that he proclaimed. By what he said and what he was, he fortified and uplifted those among whom he dwelt. Humanity transcended inhumanity. As one Catholic priest who was with him bore witness: "He achieved his greatest ministry there—among the despairing, who lived in the very shadow of death. Without him, we could not have endured."

Aged 72, he was then taken to Harteim Castle, Linz, where he was gassed for being judged "unworthy of life". Ironically, the castle had been a sanatorium for the old and infirm. The Nazis had converted it into a euthanasia centre to dispose of physically infirm prisoners from the concentration camps, as well as handicapped adults and children from institutions caring for the disabled. Death, however, held no fear for him:

If death were the end of everything, then life would be the stupidest of all comedies and would lack all meaning or purpose. . . . How could Providence abandon and betray us when our lips have barely touched the rim of the cup of life?

The castle has now, however, become a symbol of hope for the vulnerable. It is a memorial for promoting "wert des lebens" ("the value of life") for people with disabilities. In its meditation centre there is a glass box of about 30,000 river stones collected by children. Each stone represents the soul of someone murdered in Harteim.

The Flower Communion is unique, since Capek stressed the simple rule that in the Church no rituals should be appropriated from other churches or traditions. Instead, the Church should sustain "living symbols": creating and also replacing symbols that have become obsolete. So, the Flower Communion is our very own communion. It has stood the test of time since Capek devised it almost one hundred years ago. It has lasted so long because it reflects the basic character of human nature; people's unique diversity and yet also their unity. It symbolises all of us sharing the common gift of life and realising that the collective whole is far greater than its individual parts. Our Flower Communion emphasises the universality of human nature and equality before God.

Let us end with words from a meditation written by Capek in Dachau:

Outside let lightening reign
Horrible darkness frighten the world
But from the depths of your own soul
From that silence will arise again
God's flower.......
Return to yourself
Rest in yourself
Live in the depth of your soul
Where the divine and the human meet.

Sources cited in this chapter

Richard Henry. *Norbert Fabian Capek: A Spiritual Journey*. Skinner House, 1999.

Alden Nowlan. 'Sacrament'.

11 A Spiritual Spoke in the Wheel of Evil

The blood of martyrs might once again be demanded, but this blood, if we really have the courage and loyalty to shed it, will not be innocent, shining like that of the first witnesses for the faith. On our blood lies heavy guilt, the guilt of the unprofitable servant who is cast into outer darkness.
(Dietrich Bonhoeffer)

A huge moral test for established churches and individual Christians is posed if their countries are taken over by totalitarian regimes. Do they continue to follow faithfully the teachings of Jesus even when these collide with the edicts of the regime, or do the churches submit to the regime in order to secure the preservation of their authority? And in what circumstances is an individual Christian justified in attempting to overthrow a tyrannical regime? These questions starkly arose with the Nazification of Germany. Life-and-death choices had to be made; the survival of the churches – or their closure? A safe pastorate or death in a concentration camp?

Such choices are magnified in the life story of Dietrich Bonhoeffer. It was a journey during which a prayerful Lutheran theologian from a middle-class ivory tower ended up stripped naked and hung like a piece of meat by the Nazis in an extermination camp. But it is also a spiritual journey of someone who lived a well-ordered life teaching the Word of God but at the end described himself as a "non-religious Christian".

Bonhoeffer was raised in a secure family in what was then a self-contained, rule-based world. This world was to be shattered by the advent of the First World War. Both Roman Catholic and Lutheran pastors preached "God is with us". But in reality, the old order had collapsed, the Kaiser was exiled, traditional values were being questioned, and a slab of margarine cost 20 billion marks.

When Bonhoeffer began studying theology, he felt like an outsider. He was certainly a precocious high-flier, gaining his doctorate at the early age of 21. But the cosy certainty of his bourgeois upbringing and radical, dialectical theological discourse seemed to be in totally separate and conflicting worlds. As a young student, he was torn between the two.

With the end of the Kaiser's Reich, the Protestant state church which had supported a catastrophic war had lost a good deal of its legitimacy. It was only to regain its legitimacy by becoming *de facto* the state church during the Nazi regime, and virtually an adjunct of National Socialism.

As an assistant lecturer in theology at Berlin University, Bonhoeffer gradually moved away from traditional conservatism. He attended services led by a pacifist pastor and socialist. He obtained a teaching fellowship at the Union Theological seminary in New York. Here, he found not a stultifying state church, but a thriving plethora of individual denominations. He heard the gospel preached in black churches; this was the social dynamite which challenged the bourgeois nature of the church in which he had been brought up. Here, there was no separation between intellect and gut-feeling. Here, faith took on both social and emotional dimensions. For him, it was a confusing, yet liberating, experience.

Bonhoeffer was a theologian whose deep beliefs arose from prayerfulness based on the Word of Scripture, often the Psalms. But for him it was not sufficient to simply to have read God's Word:

> *It must penetrate deep within us, like the Holy of Holies in the Sanctuary, so that we do not sin in thought, word, or deed. ... Meditation is a source of peace, of patience, and of joy; it is like a magnet that draws together all the forces in our life that make for order.*

When he returned to Germany in 1931, national socialism was taking over the country, and the dark side of the capitalist system was flouting the middle-class humanistic ideals championed by the Bonhoeffer family. He saw that "our previous ordered life has been broken up and dissolved in these present days, and we are in danger of losing our inner sense of order".

The traumatic events in Germany were now pushing him into making a choice: silent conformity as a cog in the Nazi state wheel – or political resistance as a spoke in that wheel. Bonhoeffer asked whether humanity's increasing ability to cope with its problems without relying on the hypothesis of God might not indicate the obsolescence of the "religious premise" upon which Christianity had hitherto been based. He asserted that the church ought to affirm man's maturity in a "world come of age". The stripping off of "religion", in the sense of otherworldliness and preoccupation with personal salvation, would in fact free Christianity for its authentic this-worldliness, in accordance with its Judaic roots. The church should give up its inherited privileges in order to free Christians to "share in God's sufferings in the world" in imitation of Jesus, "the man for others".

When the Nazis took control of Germany in 1933, difficult choices had to be made by the churches and their clergy. Bonhoeffer had returned to New York, but he realised, when Hitler was made Chancellor, that he had fled from the evil that was taking control of his country. So, he returned, almost immediately. His first act of resistance was a radio broadcast questioning the role of the Führer. He was not arguing against the need for a strong leader but against a situation whereby a leader allowed himself to become an idol and abuse his position of leadership. The broadcast was banned by the authorities.

In July 1933, just six months after Hitler was appointed Chancellor, the Catholic Church signed the *Reichskonkordat* with Hitler, agreeing not to oppose the political and social aims of the Nazi Party. Pope Pius XI hoped that the concordat would allow the Catholic Church in Germany to operate free from interference. The concordat was not worth the paper it was written on. An attempt was even made to ban the display of crucifixes in Roman Catholic schools. From 1936 parents were pressured to withdraw their children from Catholic schools and place them in Nazi-approved schools. By 1939, most Catholic-based schools had been closed.

The Lutheran Evangelical Church, meanwhile, adopted a supine approach to the decrees of the Third Reich. It became the Reich church – the majority of the three million Nazi Party members being Protestants. The future Bishop of Berlin opined:

> *When the life or death of the nation is at stake, state power must be used thoroughly and powerfully. We have learnt from Luther that the church may not get in the way of legitimate state force if it is doing that to which it is called. Not even if it acts harshly and ruthlessly.*

Luther, it should be noted, was an anti-Semite in the fifteenth century.

The state was exercising its office in the name of God. This suited Hitler, since it gave theological ballast to a Pagan and anti-Semitic ideology. To him, Jesus was an Aryan fighter who struggled against the power and pretensions of the corrupt Pharisees and Jewish materialism. The role of the church was to persuade the state to guarantee that it could continue to preach the gospel, not necessarily to stand by the victims of the state. This view of the state was contradicted by Bonhoeffer:

> *The church can ask the state whether its actions are legitimate and it can throw the state back on its responsibilities. Secondly, it can aid the victims of state action even if they do not belong to the Christian community. The third possibility is not just to bandage the victims under the wheel, but to put a spoke in the wheel itself.*

This stemmed from his steadfast commitment to the demands set out in the Sermon on the Mount:

> *Blessed are you when people insult you, persecute you and falsely say all kinds of evil against you because of me. Rejoice and be glad, because great is your reward in heaven, for in the same way they persecuted the prophets who were before you.*

The Lutheran Church, however, had assumed that the aim of Sermon on the Mount was only to make us feel how sinful we are, since its demands were so impossibly great. It was therefore easy to argue that they could be suspended when the state required them to be cast aside: a case of suspended belief. Bonhoeffer, however, believed that the sermon was actually what Christ wanted us to practise in the real world.

How then did he try to respond to these demands in such harrowing circumstances? He was the first pastor to state that the church could not stand by and say nothing about the laws that determined the fate of the Jews. His family helped some Jews to escape the Nazi tyranny: "*Only he who cries out for the Jews may sing the Gregorian chants*".

Bonhoeffer also played an important part in the world ecumenical movement. He helped to found the Confessional Church (the *Bekennende Kirche*) as an alternative to the German Christians who had taken over the Evangelical Church, whose creed now was "One people, one Reich, one Führer, one church". The founding principles of the Confessional Church was the Barmen Declaration, drafted by the Swiss theologian, Karl Barth. It was hardly radical – stipulating that the state should not fulfil the task of the Church, and vice versa, and rejecting its subordination to the state. It was not about undermining the state and it was not proactive in defending the Jews. It was exclusively opposed to the heresies and violent measures of the German Christians within their church. It soon, however, disintegrated when all pastors had to take an oath of allegiance to the Führer or forfeit their position.

Bonhoeffer did not see himself as a hero. When he was ordered by his superior in the church not to officiate at the funeral of his Jewish brother-in-law, he obeyed the order – but felt enormous guilt about it for years afterwards. This was in contrast to the stance of his 90-year-old grandmother, who once forced a group of brown shirts blocking the entrance of a Jewish shop to get out of the way so that she could buy strawberries.

Bonhoeffer faced a huge moral question: which was the greater guilt, that of tolerating the Hitler dictatorship or that of removing it? Was anyone who was not prepared to kill Hitler guilty of mass murder? Bonhoeffer could have justified such action by quoting Psalm 58:

> *The righteous will be glad when they see vengeance; they will bathe their feet in the blood of the wicked. And they will say, "Surely, there is a reward for the righteous".*

He did not, however, want this "psalm of vengeance" to be his prayer, as "we are too sinful, too evil for it": "How then should we, who are guilty ourselves and deserving of God's wrath, call down God's vengeance upon our enemies?" According to the Gospel of Matthew, Jesus taught his followers "to love your enemies and pray for those who persecute you, that you may be sons of your Father in heaven".

Another moral issue to consider was that of likely retribution and any collateral damage. In 1942 the assassination of the Reich Protector Reinhard Heydrich by the Czech resistance resulted in 1,300 innocent civilians being murdered and the village of Lidice raised to the ground.

Ultimately, however, Bonhoeffer was prepared to make a giant leap and to join an attempt on Hitler's life in order to prevent millions more people being sacrificed on the altar of Nazism:

> *Freedom comes from deeds, not through thoughts taking wing ... No one who confines himself to the limits of duty ever goes so far as to venture, on his sole responsibility, to act in the only way that makes it possible to score a direct hit on evil and defeat it ... We must set the firebrand of truth to all corners of the proud German Christian edifice so that one day the whole structure may collapse.*

But before he could take such action, he would have to leave the Church, as any use of force would be contrary to his former stance. Circumstances now demanded that a good Christian become a state criminal.

A unique opportunity to undermine the regime came when Bonhoeffer was recruited to serve in the Abwehr as a courier, where a brother-in-law was employed. It was the office for spying and counter espionage, under the supreme command of the Wehrmacht. Like his brother-in-law, he became a double agent, passing information about Nazi atrocities to the Allies. When they were discovered, they were arrested and tried by a so-called People's Court and imprisoned.

It was the last attempt on Hitler's life, led by Colonel von Stauffenberg, that sealed Dietrich's fate and that of the Abwehr members of the resistance. The order was made that all be hanged for high treason – just a month before Germany conceded military defeat. He was hanged at Flossenbürg extermination camp on 9 April 1945, within the sound of the guns of the American liberators.

So, Bonhoeffer did not live to see how the majority of German Christians felt no guilt over the concentration camps, euthanasia programmes, and genocide, and how after the fall of the Nazi regime almost all its pastors would remain in office, presumably preaching the Sermon on the Mount. His last words were:

> *This the end, for me the beginning of life. I believe in universal Christian brotherhood which rises above national interests and I believe that our victory is certain.*

The road to the concentration camps had been his road to Damascus. It was here that he communed and found solidarity with men who were not of his class, race, or faith; some were communists. He had, for once, viewed from below "the excluded, maltreated, powerless, oppressed and scorned". His otherworldliness had been transcended into inworldliness. He had believed that he "could acquire faith by trying to live a holy life" but now recognised that "it is only by living completely in this world that one learns to have faith". Ordered religion had long abandoned him and he had become a Christian martyr, religion-less yet true to Christ's teaching.

Sources cited in this chapter

Bonhoeffer, Dietrich. *Meditating on the Word.* Cowley Publications, 2000.

Renate Wind. *Dietrich Bonhoeffer: A Spoke in the Wheel.* Wm. Eerdmans Publishing, 1992.

12 Liberating the Oppressed

> *We will have an authentic theology of liberation only when the oppressed themselves can freely raise their voice and express themselves directly and creatively in society and in the heart of the People of God.*
> (Father Gustavo Gutiérrez)

Liberation theology is about fighting poverty by addressing its alleged source: sin. It forges a radical relationship between Christian (especially Roman Catholic) theology and political activism, particularly in relation to economic justice, poverty, and human rights. It is radical, in that it sees theology from the perspective of the poor and the oppressed, tackling it not just through intercessional prayer to a God above, but through collective social action from below.

The best-known form of liberation theology is that which developed within the Catholic Church in Latin America in the 1950s and 1960s, arising principally as a moral reaction to the poverty and social injustice in the region. Such injustice was rooted in the Spanish conquest of Peru and Mexico in the sixteenth century by Spanish conquistadors such as Pizarro and Cortes respectively. It had resulted in the destruction of the Inca and Aztec civilisations. Actively supported by religious orders such as the Franciscans, the conquistadors imposed Catholicism on Latin America, introducing mass baptisms of the indigenous population and creating above them a privileged class of those of Spanish descent. Almost 40 per cent of the world's Roman Catholics now live in South America, and the present pope is Argentinian.

The term 'liberation theology' was coined in 1971 by the Peruvian Dominican priest, Gustavo Gutiérrez, who wrote one of the movement's defining books, *A Theology of Liberation*. It is a scholarly book, but his theology comes from real experience – living and working among the poor in a Lima slum. He defines such theology as a "faith based on the commitment to abolish injustice and to build a new society"; perhaps to build Jerusalem in those dark Satanic slums. It involves "a commitment to effective participation in the struggle which the exploited classes have undertaken against their oppressors".

Liberation theology can be interpreted as an attempt to return to the gospel of the early church in places where Christianity is politically and culturally decentralised. It could be said that concern for the poor and the oppressed was central to the teachings of Jesus Christ. When he came to Nazareth, Jesus went to the synagogue on the Sabbath day. He stood up to read from the scroll of the prophet Isaiah:

> *The Spirit of the Lord is upon me, because he has anointed me to bring good news to the poor. He has sent me to proclaim release to the captives and recovery of sight to the blind, to let the oppressed go free, to proclaim the year of the Lord's favour.*

Perhaps Jesus was assuring the poor and oppressed that they would be fed and freed in the afterlife, obviating the need to take action to do this during their time on this earth. Nevertheless, he is not passive. He admonishes the oppressor:

> *Whoever oppresses a poor man insults his Maker, but he who is generous to the needy honours Him.*

Luke's Gospel states: "Blessed are you poor, for yours is the Kingdom of God". Gutiérrez believes that this is not an eschatological promise: an inducement to accept your poverty in this life because later the injustice will be compensated for in the kingdom of God. Such a promise has for centuries justified the status qu,o as in the Victorian Anglican hymn:

> *The rich man in his castle,*
> *The poor man at his gate,*
> *God made them, high or lowly*
> *And ordered their estate.*

Gutiérrez regards poverty as an evil and therefore incompatible with the Kingdom of God. He quotes from the Gospel of Mark: "The time has come; the Kingdom of God is upon you". He believes that the Kingdom already exists on this earth, and that the elimination of the exploitation and poverty that "prevent the poor from being fully human" has begun:

> *They [the poor] are blessed because the coming of the Kingdom will put an end to their poverty by creating a world of fellowship. They are blessed because the Messiah will open the eyes of the blind and will give bread to the hungry.*

Liberation theology sprang from the outcomes of the conference of Latin American Catholic bishops in Medellín, Colombia in 1968. It chose the "Reign of God" over the status and security of the institutional Church. The bishops rolled the dice, so to speak, in favour of the values of God's kingdom, risking the historical power and prestige that the Church had enjoyed in that part of the world for centuries. The phrase "preferential option for the poor" came to summarise the bishops' challenge to the entire household of faith in Latin America. Theology should not be a debate about how many angels can dance on the head of a pin, but a question of how many people can be saved from poverty and oppression. It is a call for humanistic, pastoral, and collective social action. A major outcome from the conference was Gutiérrez's *A Theology of Liberation.*

Such theology, however, has been a very contestable concept. The Vatican rejected certain forms of Latin American liberation theology for focusing on institutionalised or systemic sin, as opposed to individual sin. It also rejected the identification of the Catholic Church hierarchy in South America as members of the same privileged class that had long been oppressing indigenous populations. Liberation theology contends that the Church must assume some responsibility for the injustice that it has supported by its links with the established order, as well as by its silence regarding the evils that this order implies.

Pope John Paul II criticised radical liberation theology, saying, "This idea of Christ as a political figure, a revolutionary, as the subversive of Nazareth, does not tally with the Church's catechesis". He did, however, acknowledge that "the growing wealth of a few parallels the growing poverty of the masses". He affirmed both the principle of private property and the challenge to the Church to "preach, educate individuals and communities, form public opinion, and offer orientations to the leaders of the peoples" towards the goal of a "more just and equitable distribution of goods":

> *The social doctrine is not a third way between liberal capitalism and Marxist collectivism. It constitutes a category of its own...the field of moral theology.*

The election of Pope Francis as the first pontiff from South America has, perhaps, proved to be a turning point: he is someone who has emphasised the central importance of eradicating poverty. He has not, however, embraced liberation theology unconditionally in its entirety, and has eschewed any Marxist interpretation of the gospels. But he is sympathetic to its basic premises, believing that social inequality and increasing poverty are caused by economic neoliberalism; he prefers, instead, economic systems characterised by a higher intervention by the state. In 2018 Pope Francis wished Gustavo Gutiérrez a happy 90th birthday as the "father of liberation theology" and thanked him for his contributions to the Catholic Church and his love for the poor.

The Medellín conference was a sea-change for the Church and had far-reaching effects. Within ten years, a thousand pastoral ministers – mostly lay preachers – had suffered martyrdom for the "crime" of implementing the pastoral guidelines set out in its documents. Those guidelines not only challenged and shook church structures, but more importantly questioned and subverted the terribly unjust status quo of Latin American societies. These structures had trapped the vast majority of people in what Pope Paul VI had called "the vicious cycle of poverty." Oscar Romero was such a martyr. As Archbishop of San Salvador, he spoke out against poverty, social injustice, assassinations, and torture amid a growing war between leftist rebels and government and right-wing forces. In 1980, Romero was assassinated by a right-wing death squad while celebrating Mass in the chapel of the Hospital of Divine Providence. He died at the foot of the crucifix and was later canonised as a saint by Pope Francis.

Latin American liberation theology also met opposition in the United States. It was seen as a challenge to US neo-colonialism in the subcontinent. The CIA funded various conservative groups throughout Latin America such as Opus Dei, which had a strong affinity to military regimes and even supported attempted right-wing coups. The CIA warned of Liberation Theology's deliberate exploitation "by Marxist-Leninist groups to promote revolutionary change" by seeking a just life now, not in the hereafter, by means of violence. President Ronald Reagan even summoned a National Security Council meeting to address its "threat".

One of Liberal Theology's proponents in the USA was Dorothy Day. Although she opposed US intervention in countries such as Nicaragua and supported the Cuban revolution under Castro, she eschewed violence. Her deep pacifism was based on the Sermon on the Mount: she took no sides on the Spanish Civil War, did not support the USA joining the Second World War after Pearl Harbour, and campaigned against military conscription. She also called for people to do penance for dropping the atomic bomb on Hiroshima and Nagaski.

> *The citizen is obliged in conscience not to follow the directives of civil authorities when they are contrary to the demands of the moral order, to the fundamental rights of persons or the teachings of the Gospel.*

Day was born in Brooklyn, New York in 1897. Together with Peter Maurin, she founded the Catholic Worker movement and published its newspaper. As a student, she joined the Socialist Party and came to embrace Marx's belief that religion was merely an opiate of the people, invented to help them endure their suffering and to accept the injustices of the capitalist system. She actively opposed the First World War and was a lifelong pacifist. Day was also a suffragist who was imprisoned for picketing the White House and went on hunger strike. During that time in prison, she said that she "clung to words of comfort in the Bible":

> *Yet all the while I read, my pride was fighting on. I did not want to go to God in defeat and sorrow. I was like a child that wants to walk by itself. I kept brushing away the hand that held me up.*

But then among her close friends – socialists and anarchists – she began to pray, developing a deepening relationship with God. She then became pregnant by her lover, a naturalist and anarchist. She had been forced to have an abortion five years earlier at the insistence of another lover. But even though this second lover also did not want to see himself as a father, Dorothy gave birth to the child and brought her up herself.

In 1932, Day was hired by a Jesuit magazine to report on the hunger march in Washington DC, protesting about the conditions of the unemployed. The press portrayed them as a communist attempt to seize the capital, and the police threw tear gas at them and beat up the leaders. Day questioned the Church's lack of support for the unemployed:

> *I could protest, to arouse the conscience, but where was the Catholic leadership in the gathering of bands of men and women together, for the actual works of mercy that comrades had always made part of their technique in reaching the workers?*

It was when she met her mentor, Peter Maurin, that her religious faith and political conscience gradually conjoined with social action. In Maurin's view:

> *Catholic scholars have taken the dynamite of the church; they have wrapped it up in nice phraseology, have placed it in a hermetically sealed container and sat on the lid. It is about time to take the lid off and to make the Catholic dynamite dynamic.*

He held the view that both communism and capitalism failed to promote a society in which individuals can realise a truly human life. This reflected the encyclical of Pope Pius XI on the condition of the working class in which the twin rocks of shipwreck – individualism and collectivism – had to be avoided.

The Catholic Worker movement was established not as a political movement but rather as a spiritual movement that would address the problems facing society. Its social programme included reaching the man in the street with social teachings of the Church. It founded houses of hospitality for the practice of the spiritual works of mercy and established farming communes to alleviate unemployment. Dorothy Day lived, worked, and prayed in these houses and farms.

Her ability to see Jesus Christ in all those she met, particularly in those who were outcasts of society, was the centre of her spirituality. She always claimed that one should not serve the poor out of duty but out of the love of Christ, whom they embody. It is not a duty to serve Christ: it is a privilege.

> *All Christians are called to be hospitable. But it is more than serving a meal or filling a bed, opening the door – it is to open ourselves, our hearts to the needs of others.*

It would be wrong to view Day as someone from the radical left who became a dissenting Catholic. She did, of course, come from the left, but she loved the Church and was obedient to it, as is the case of most converts who choose the faith and are not born into it. To her, obedience was a matter of love. For example, she always expressed her support for the Church's teachings on sexuality, chastity, birth control, and abortion.

Towards the end of her life, Dorothy told people: "Don't call me a saint, I don't want to be dismissed that easily". Since her death in 1980, the Church has contemplated her canonisation. But perhaps her most important legacy are her writings and the houses of hospitality that continue to put her spiritual beliefs into practice.

In an historic address to the US Congress, Pope Francis stated that her "social activism, her passion for justice and for the cause of the oppressed were inspired by the Gospel, her faith, and the example of the saints". He held her up as a model for the world to follow by giving hope to the oppressed; and he bestowed on her the accolade, "Servant of God".

Now, nearly half a century since the Medellín conference and its aftermath, one must ask if the spirit of liberation theology is still alive in a world drowning in neo-liberalism. Father Joe Frangle, a Franciscan friar, feels that, despite a perhaps inevitable mitigation of the cutting-edge nature of that spirit, Medellín still lives. It has soaked into the soil – the DNA – of the Church at the grass-roots in Latin America. More broadly, the vision of a "preferential option for the poor" has spread to other areas of church life as well. Virtually every religious congregation of women and men in the world has in one way or another called its members to make such a commitment, personally and corporately. Like the Second Vatican Council itself, which addressed relations between the Church and the modern world, Medellín can no more be forgotten or suppressed than can toothpaste be put back into the tube. Its Liberation Theology has been a precious and progressive gift from the Latin American Church to the universal church.

Sources cited in this chapter

Day, Dorothy. *The Long Loneliness: The Autobiography*. Harper San Francisco, 1997.

Gustavo Gutiérrez. *A Theology of Liberation*. SCM Press, 1988.

Terence C Wright. *Dorothy Day: An Introduction to Her Life and Thought*. Ignatius Press, 2018.

13 God in the Trenches

Men fought like brutes; and hideous things were done,
And you have nourished hatred harsh and blind.
But in that Golgotha perhaps you'll find
The mothers of the men who killed your son.
(Siegfried Sassoon)

Whether killing a fellow human is ever justified has been argued within the Abrahamic faiths ever since Moses brought the tablets of stone down from the mountain. The commandment "thou shalt not kill" was "written with the finger of God". It can be narrowly interpreted as a directive to an individual or, more widely, to a state. After the Second World War, state leaders have been tried for mass killings and crimes against peace and humanity. As the philosopher Michael Walzer has said: "war is the hardest place: if comprehensive and consistent moral judgements are possible there, they are possible everywhere".

The early church was strongly pacifist, in accordance with the teachings of Jesus in the Sermon on the Mount:

Blessed are the peacemakers, for they shall be called sons of God. Blessed are you when others revile you and persecute you and utter all kinds of evil against you falsely on my account. Rejoice and be glad, for your reward is great in heaven, for so they persecuted the prophets who were before you.

The Christian theologian, Clement of Alexandria, wrote that "he who holds the sword must cast it away and if one of the faithful becomes a soldier he must be rejected by the Church, for he has scorned God". This view changed rapidly in the time of the Roman emperor, Constantine. The bishops' Council of Arles in 314 stated that to forbid "the state the right to go to war was to condemn it to extinction" and they even called for conscientious objectors to military service to be excommunicated.

Almost 100 million souls perished in both world wars. The statistics of the audit of war are almost impossible to imagine. The slaughter was on an industrial scale. In the First World War, 19 million died, and in the Second World War almost 80 million died. Almost two-thirds of these deaths were those of non-combatants. The Four Horsemen of the Apocalypse-war, death, pestilence and famine- had galloped into the twentieth century.

Those losses touched most families. My two great-uncles were killed in the First World War. Corporal Joe Brown of the 7th Battalion East Yorkshire Regiment was killed aged 26 in December 1917, dying from his wounds in his native Liverpool. His brother, Private Jim Brown, of the Black Watch Highlanders, was killed in Flanders aged 22, four months later, and buried, in Rupert Brooke's words "in some corner of a foreign field that is forever England". My grandmother throughout her long life never mentioned the demise of her two brothers. Perhaps she buried her grief with them.

How then should we as Unitarians address the moral and ethical issues raised by war? The early Christians were inclined to pacifism, based on the teaching of Jesus: "Blessed are the peacemakers, for they will be called the children of God". By enduring violence, you could look forward to a reward beyond this world. This pacifism remains a thread in modern Christianity, particularly among the Quakers. "Would Jesus have bayonetted a German soldier?" asked Alfred Salter, Quaker, doctor, and pacifist Labour MP.

The moral quandary is highlighted when the soldier realises that the foe is not just an enemy but a human being. Human compassion transcending brutal nationalism is the subject of *All Quiet on the Western Front* by the German novelist, Erich Maria Remarque:

> *Comrade, I did not want to kill you...But you were only an idea to me before; an abstraction that lived in my mind and called forth an appropriate response. It was that abstraction I stabbed. But now, for the first time, I see you are a man like me. I thought of your hand-grenades, of your bayonets, of your rifle; now I see your wife and your face and our fellowship...forgive me, comrade; how could you be my enemy?*

A friend of mine, Bob Hockley, who was also a Quaker, socialist, and pacifist, felt himself to be in no such quandary. Bob was a carpenter whose beard made him look positively Christ-like. In 1942, he pleaded guilty to refusing to take a medical examination. He did so because it was likely that it would have deemed him unfit for military service due to his poor eyesight. That would have prevented him from being registered as a conscious objector. At the tribunal hearing, he renounced war, citing quotations from the Bible and the Quaker Peace Testimony. He was sentenced to six months' hard labour in Wormwood Scrubs for, in his words, "refusing to kill a fellow human being".

Saint Augustine differentiated between individual killing (which was a sin) and killing on the authority of a monarch or God himself. He argued that warfare was an inescapable part of the human condition and might be a tragic necessity: if it was conducted in order to minimise the consequences of sin, it was therefore a just action. This belief was, however, swept away by the fervours of the Crusades. They were a kind of penitential holy war – waged on behalf of God; Christians against Muslims; good versus evil – in which all moral restraint was abandoned.

The belief was only restored by St Thomas Aquinas in the thirteenth century, who developed the concept of the "Just War". It embraced the concepts of last resort, the weighing of good versus evil, assessing whether there would be a reasonable hope of success, and the use of legitimate means. Innocent people and non-combatants should not be harmed, and only appropriate force should be used. A similar concept had been developed in the Islamic world. Warfare was allowable if it was conducted to protect – but not to promote – the practice of Islam. Right intention excluded personal benefit. This was the very opposite of the Crusaders' self-justified aim to impose Christianity on Muslim states by force through so-called "Holy Wars".

The 'Just-War' theory has two sets of criteria: *jus ad bellum*: the right to go to war; and *jus in bello*: right conduct within war. Michael Walzer believes that the two sorts of judgement are logically independent. It is perfectly possible for a just war to be fought unjustly (for example, via the mass bombing of civilians), and for an unjust war to be fought in strict accordance with the Geneva Convention (for example, to protect prisoners of war).

War is a military extension of politics, and Unitarians generally agree that we must find better ways to resolve conflicts and disputes. Some believe that war can never be justified in any situation; but many believe that it should be used only as a last resort and used proportionately. There are extreme situations in which the use of proportionate force is necessary in order to prevent or defeat a greater evil – particularly to defend the innocent and the weak from immediate peril.

Meeting the *jus ad bellum* criterion provided legitimacy for the Allies entering the Second World War to prevent the devastation wrought by Nazi and Japanese militarism. It is, however, questionable whether it equally applied to the First World War. The philosopher, Bertrand Russell, was shunned by the Establishment for opposing the First World War and was accordingly dismissed from his Cambridge fellowship. In old age, he reflected that it would have been very much better for the world if Britain had remained neutral and Germany had won a quick victory. This might well have averted the mass destruction that Nazism and Communism were to inflict on the world twenty years later in the wake of so-called Armageddon, "the war to end all wars".

In the First World War, we can see British troops blessed by chaplains and German troops blessed by Lutheran pastors. Apparently God was on both sides of the trenches. Every soldier had a Bible, and many were seen clutching on to it as they lay mortally wounded in no-man's land. There were few atheists in trenches under fire. Like many of his generation, the poet Rupert Brooke saw the outbreak of the war as an opportunity to cleanse his soul. Another poet, Wilfred Owen, who was killed in 1918 after being awarded the Military Cross, felt it was "not sweet and right to die for your country":

If you could hear, at every jolt, the blood
Come gargling from the froth-corrupted lungs,
Obscene as cancer, bitter as the cud
Of vile, incurable sores on innocent tongues, –
My friend, you would not tell with such high zest
To children ardent for some desperate glory,
The old Lie: Dulce et decorum est
Pro patria mori.

The Chilean poet, Pablo Neruda, who was a communist and atheist, views religion as being used for political than spiritual ends and hollowed out like "empty shells of a mollusc".

What we came across in these blood thirsty times
With their smoke of burning trash, their dead ashes
As we weren't able to stop looking
We often stopped to look at the names of God
We lifted them with tenderness because they reminded us
Of our ancestors, of the first people, those who said the prayers
Those who discovered the hymn that united them in misfortune
And now seeing the empty fragments which sheltered those ancient people
We feel those smooth substances,
Worn out and used up by good and by evil.
Guatama Christ by Pablo Neruda

Difficult ethical decisions have to be made during wars. In the Second World War, Churchill ordered the scuttling of the fleet of our French allies off the Algerian coast to prevent it from being commandeered by the Germans. Almost 1,300 French seamen were sacrificed. Parliament unanimously approved of the action, but the decision haunted Churchill for the rest of his life.

Towards the end of the Second World War mass destruction could be activated by a B-29 pilot just pressing a release button. The atomic bomb, "Little Boy", killed 80,000 Japanese civilians at Hiroshima – presumably including many little boys. A second bomb killed 40,000 at Nagasaki. Many more died of radiation sickness in the aftermath of the bombings. There is a powerful argument that such targeting of non-combatants, in the knowledge that the casualty rate would be excessive in relation to the anticipated advantage, did not meet the *jus in bello* criterion.

The stockpiling of nuclear weapons during the Cold War led to a huge ethical debate on their use. In 1983, the US Catholic bishops asserted that good ends such as the defence of one's country and its freedom cannot justify immoral means such as the use of weapons that kill indiscriminately and threaten whole societies. Peace-making is not an optional commitment, the bishops said. It is a requirement of our faith. In the UK, the Campaign for Nuclear Disarmament (CND) had considerable support from Christians. The Anglican priest, Canon Collins, was a founder of CND; he had also set up Christian Action to work for reconciliation with Germany after the Second World War.

In 1985, the General Assembly of the Unitarian Universalist Association in the USA passed a resolution which sought an end to the nuclear arms race:

> *Believing that humankind is free to choose life, we denounce the blasphemy against life which is represented by the development, production, deployment and threatened use of nuclear weapons. Pledging, in our religious principles, to protect the Earth and interdependence of its living system, we choose to create hope and the vision of a better world. We fulfil this pledge through our efforts to abolish all nuclear weapons from the face of the earth.*

If we are not all Unitarian pacifists and against all warfare, then we need to apply the test: is the conflict in question just – or not? Which side is sufficiently right, and are the values at stake critical enough to override the moral prescription against war and justify killing? Will the proposed action protect innocent life or secure basic human rights? Have all the peaceful alternatives been exhausted? Are the damage to be inflicted and the costs incurred proportionate to the good outcomes expected by taking up arms? It is an ethical risk analysis. It is easier, however, with the benefit of hindsight, to assess the justness of war after the conflict has ended than before it begins.

If we consider the Falklands War, then we find that about 255 British troops and 649 Argentinian troops were killed, and 1,800 wounded, in the British defence of the freedom of fewer than 3,000 inhabitants in a remote island 8,000 miles away. If we had not gone to war, would the Argentinian dictatorship have killed or wounded that number of islanders? But again hindsight is a wonderful thing. Patriotism often trumps compassion. At a memorial service for those killed in Iraq at St Paul's Cathedral, the then Archbishop of Canterbury was afterwards admonished by the Conservative ministers as unpatriotic for preaching that it was a Christian duty to pray for the dead of both sides.

The war in Iraq mounted by a coalition led by George W Bush, a God-fearing Methodist, and Tony Blair, a devout Anglo-Catholic, was on a much larger scale. Perhaps they also saw it as a coalition between the Mighty and The Almighty. Feelings against the invasion were high. More than a million people demonstrated against it in London. Pope John Paul II reminded us that Iraq was the "land of the prophets" and that "war was never a means for settling differences between nations". The Church of England issued its Mothers' Union prayer to world leaders, in an attempt to deter them from declaring war on the grounds that "nobody has total power over any country or its people but God alone".

The rationale for invading Iraq was the need for regime change from a Sunni dictatorship to a pro-West liberal democracy. The moral shield was the mistaken belief that Saddam Hussein had weapons of mass destruction which could be launched within 45 minutes against the West. The invasion might have satisfied the criterion of *jus ad bellum* if such weapons had actually existed. It is, however, highly questionable whether invasion of a country to change its governing regime, even if that regime had been responsible for the killing and oppression of hundreds of thousands of its innocent citizens, would be a just war. According to Walzer, the Just-War theory is about the restoration of the *status quo ante.* It is certainly about eliminating a state's capacity to mount future aggression, but not about transforming a totalitarian regime into a democracy; the single exception being the Nazi state.

As Blair has stated: "We want our battles short and successful....if they turn out to be bloodied, protracted and uncertain, our will weakens". Saddam's toppling was certainly rapid, but its aftermath was bloody and protracted, resulting in a failed state riven by sectarianism and human suffering. The mortality statistics of the Iraq invasion are stark: about 500,000 Iraqis died – mainly civilians – while around 5,000 invading troops were killed. More than a million people were displaced. The maths tells us that the damage inflicted and the costs to human life incurred were grossly disproportionate to the outcome of toppling Saddam Hussein's regime. Nor had there been any planning to address the dire consequences of the aftermath. The test of *Jus in bello* had not been met.

Blair has said that "you don't put a hotline up to God and get the answers". His Christian faith did not cause his intervention, but it was a key part of his moral outlook for re-ordering the world that made it possible. Counter-intuitively, it contributed to increasing disorder in the Middle East. As the former Archbishop Rowan Williams has said of Blair, "he is strong on God but very weak on irony".

Walzer warns of the limitations of the "democratic idealism" which was used to "legitimise" Bush's crusade against the "axis of evil": North Korea, Iran, and Iraq:

> *What is objectionable about democratic idealism, as the realists call it, is that it sets goals that cannot possibly be reached, for which soldiers can only die in vain. This is a moral objection, and an important one if soldiers have in fact been asked to die for such purposes as "the eradication of evil". Their most heroic effort, after all, can only bring a particular war to an end; they cannot end war. They can save democracy from a particular threat, but they cannot make the world safe for democracy.*

What is also important to us Unitarians is what happens after hostilities end: the reconciliation that is essential for sustaining peace. One night in 1940, Coventry suffered terrible bombardment by 500 enemy aircraft. More than 4,000 homes were destroyed, 350 civilians were killed, and the fourteenth-century cathedral destroyed. Four years later, the Allied high command decided to "coventrate" Dresden by blanket bombing – lasting not one night but several weeks. At least 35,000 civilians were killed – one hundred times more than those in Coventry. Was this an appropriate use of force – or just a bid for revenge? Even Churchill questioned the decision afterwards.

But a phoenix arose out of the ashes of Coventry and Dresden. The ruins of Coventry Cathedral still stand, next to the rebuilt cathedral designed by Basil Spence. "Father Forgive" is engraved on the ruins. This is where the German-born pacifist, Canon Paul Oestreicher, set up the Centre for International Reconciliation. Dresden's Cathedral has also been rebuilt. A gold cross on the building was made by a London goldsmith whose father had flown as a bomber pilot over Dresden.

The only phoenix arising out of the ashes of war and oppression is that of reconciliation. In the words of Nelson Mandela:

> *No-one is born hating another person because of his or her race or religion. People must learn to hat. They can, however, be taught to love, for love comes more naturally to the human heart than its opposite.*

As he walked out of the prison door at Robbin Island towards the gate that would lead to his freedom, Mandela knew that "if I didn't leave my bitterness and hatred behind, I would still be in prison".

Sources cited in this chapter

Tony Blair. *A Journey*. Hutchinson, 2010.

Robert Hockley. *Beyond the Next Hill*. Published by Robert Hockley, 1998.

Michael Walzer. *Just and Unjust Wars: A Moral Argument with Historical Illustrations*. Basic Books, 1992.

14 Hell on Earth

> *Never shall I forget those moments that murdered my God and my soul and turned my dreams to ashes. Never shall I forget those things, even if I continued to live as long as God Himself. Never.*
> (Elie Wiesel, Holocaust survivor)

One of the great imponderables of modern times is how six million Jews were allowed to be murdered in the Holocaust. In Hebrew, it is called the "Shoah", meaning "catastrophe". It was the attempt to eliminate a whole race who were described in the Book of Deuteronomy as God's "chosen people":

> *For you are a people holy to the Lord your God. The Lord your God has chosen you to be a people for his treasured possession, out of all the peoples who are on the face of the earth.*

Their suffering is unimaginable, and the reasoning for it unfathomable. Why were God's "chosen people" chosen by the Nazis for extermination and one of the oldest religions chosen for desecration? In the words of the poet Geoffrey Hill "on the ordained day, this world went spinning from Jehovah's hand".

In the Nazis' bible, *Mein Kampf*, Hitler even evoked Christianity as a reason to victimise the Jews. He did so by associating the Jewish religion with Marxism:

> *Should the Jew, with the aid of his Marxist creed, triumph over the people of this world, his Crown will be the funeral wreath of mankind. So, I believe today that my conduct is in accordance with the will of the Almighty creator – in standing guard against the Jew I am defending the handiwork of the Lord.*

Ironically, Hitler was a lapsed Catholic – indeed a very lapsed Catholic, whose regime closed churches and imprisoned and hanged numerous priests and ministers. According to the historian Alan Bullock, in Hitler's eyes "Christianity was a religion fit only for slaves; he detested its ethics in particular". Its teaching, Hitler declared, was a rebellion against the natural law of selection by struggle and the survival of the fittest. Many Nazi leaders, such as Himmler, even wanted Germans to revert to the old paganism of the early tribal Germanic gods.

The roots of Jewish victimisation lie deep in religious history. The Jew was depicted as a diabolical figure who hated Christ. He was denigrated in the legend of the "Wandering Jew"; a mythical immortal man whose legend began to spread in Europe in the thirteenth century. The original legend concerns a Jew who taunted Jesus on the way to the Crucifixion and was then cursed to walk the earth until the Second Coming.

The Lateran Council of Rome, convened by the misnamed Pope Innocent the Third in 1215, decreed that Jews must wear different clothes to distinguish them from Christians and it forbade them to hold public office. This gave religious sanction to the anti-Semitism that was rampant in medieval England. Under the Statutes of Jewry, all Jews had to pay special taxes; could not have personal relationships with Christians; could not build new synagogues; and even had to lower their voices in existing ones so that Christians could not hear the Torah being read. All Jews over the age of seven were required to wear a yellow badge. This persecution culminated in King Edward the First's Edict of Expulsion of 1290, which expelled all Jews from England – an edict which was overturned four centuries later by Oliver Cromwell. These papal edicts and state laws were mirrored in the anti-Semitic Nuremburg laws enacted seven centuries later, in 1935.

Anti-Semitism was ubiquitous in Europe as a whole. Spanish Jews who had not been forcibly converted to Christianity were expelled in 1492 through the Alhambra Edict promoted by the Inquisition. The pogroms in Tsarist Russia in the late nineteenth and early twentieth centuries also persecuted Jews. They were "justified" by a hoax document: the *Protocols of the Elders of Zion,* a fabricated text purporting to describe a Jewish plan for global domination. Although exposed by *The Times* in 1921, it was disseminated widely in the Western world by anti-Semites such as Henry Ford and used in Nazi propaganda to justify the Holocaust.

The Nuremburg Laws set out a legal framework which allowed Jews to be denigrated, isolated, dehumanised, and then exterminated. They were no longer to be German. Intermarriage and personal relationships between Aryan Germans and Jews were outlawed in order to "protect German blood and honour". For the first time in history, Jews faced persecution not for their religion but for their race. Jews who had never visited a synagogue or who had even converted to Christianity could not be classified as German and thus saved from the gas chamber.

They were forced to wear a yellow badge, stripped of their professions and businesses, thrown out of their homes, crammed into ghettos, corralled into concentration camps, starved and murdered. All of this was meticulously planned at the Wannsee conference chaired by Reinhard Heydrich and serviced by Adolf Eichmann. Plans for the industrial extermination of a race were given an innocuous name: "The Final Solution". It was to be implemented by SS officers, many of whom were university graduates. The law graduates were to kill innocent people without a trial; the medical graduates were to conduct medical experiments on children. Ironically, they themselves had been dehumanised in order to exterminate innocent people who had been classed by their political masters as "sub-humans".

This barbarism was ignored by the Lutheran Evangelical Church in Germany, whose primary objective was self-preservation and whose ministers had to take an oath of allegiance to the Reich or be dismissed (see Chapter 11). Ironically, the church had become an adjunct of an anti-religious state.

The Vatican remained politically neutral in Fascist Italy. Under the 1933 *Reichskonkordat* agreed between Pope Pius XI and Hitler, the German state would permit the practice of Catholicism, provided that it stayed out of political matters. Six years later, on the advent of war, Pope Pius XII issued an encyclical, *Summi Pontificatus,* which was a critique of both racism and totalitarianism. Such regimes "wantonly break the Tables of God's Commandments to substitute other tables and other standards stripped of the ethical content of the Revelation on Sinai, standards in which the spirit of the Sermon on the Mount and of the Cross has no place".

There has been criticism of the Vatican's low profile in denouncing anti-Semitism. But its churches were instructed to provide discreet aid and sanctuary to Jewish people, and the Vatican itself shielded many Jews. Certainly, the Nazi regime reneged on the Concordat, oppressing the churches, closing its schools, and sending many priests to their death in concentration camps.

Nevertheless, at the end of the war, Catholic priests such as the Nazi sympathiser Bishop Hudal actively supported the "ratlines". These were escape routes enabling notorious Nazis to flee to Latin America. Such anti-Semite escapees included the Holocaust planner, Adolf Eichmann; the "Angel of Death" Josef Mengele; and the Treblinka death camp commandant, Franz Stangl.

The persecution of the Jews was in some ways tragically absurd. One edict banned all Jews for having pets, all which had to be euthanised. One man was detained by the Gestapo for refusing to give up his beloved parakeet. A few weeks later, his wife received a postcard from the Gestapo informing her that for the payment of three Reichsmarks she could collect the urn containing her husband's ashes. As the French philosopher Voltaire said "Once you can get men (sic) to believe in absurdity you can get them to commit atrocities".

Wladyslaw Szpilman tells what happened to a ten-year-old boy on the street of the Warsaw ghetto. He was so scared that he forgot to take his cap off to a German policeman. The policeman drew his revolver without a word, put it to boy's temple and shot him dead. Szpilman describes him as "a placid man who had just carried out one of, his many, minor daily duties and put it out of his mind again at once, for other and more important business awaited him". It was just one of thousands of daily acts in this banality of evil.

This irrational hatred is described by the Italian Jew, Primo Levi, who survived Auschwitz:

> *There is no rationality in the Nazi hatred: it is hate that is not in us, it is outside of man [sic]. We cannot understand it, but we must understand from where it springs, and we must be on our guard. If understanding is impossible, knowing is imperative, because what happened could happen again...... The ideas they proclaimed were not always the same and were, in general, aberrant or silly or cruel. And yet they were acclaimed with hosannas and followed to the death by millions of the faithful.*

Mobs led by the SA stormtroopers trashed shops, burned books, and desecrated thousands of synagogues during Kristallnacht in November 1938. Eric Lucas, a Jewish teenager, witnessed such desecration in the German village of Hoengen:

> *Suddenly, with one loud cry of "Down with the Jews", the gathering outside produced axes and heavy sledgehammers. They stormed into the little House of God. Three men who had smashed the ark threw the Scrolls of the Law of Moses out to the screaming and shouting mass of people which had filled the little synagogue....Naked and open, the scrolls lay in the muddy autumn lane. Children stepped on them and tore pieces from the fine parchment on which the Law was written. The same law which the people who tore it apart had, in vain, tried to absorb for over a thousand years.*

The persecution of the Jews was not confined to Germans. Jewish police in the ghettos and Kapos in the camps could be as brutal as the SS. As soon as the Jewish police donned their uniforms, they shouted commands like their SS masters and beat fellow Jews with their rubber truncheons. Ukrainians, Lithuanians, and Hungarians also collaborated in the massacre of Jews. Even at the end of the War, anti-Semitic Poles prevented the few surviving Jews from returning to their homes. Some were even murdered by mobs who believed the age-old myth that Judaism was responsible for the ritual murder of children.

Life in the ghettos was horrendous, with many starving and some being murdered. Just as the pious Jew felt guilty if he missed his daily prayers, so the Gestapo policeman felt guilty if he had not beaten a Jew each day. The Leaders of the Elders which ran the ghettos faced a moral quandary. They had to collaborate with the SS to try to minimise the deportations. When the Nazis demanded that orphans and old people in the Warsaw ghetto must be deported or one hundred hostages would be killed, its Leader, Adam Czerniaków, refused to make that choice and swallowed cyanide. A similar choice faced the despotic leader of the Lodz ghetto, Chaim Rumkowski. In his notorious "Give Up Your Children" speech, he implored parents to allow 20,000 children to be sent to Chelmno extermination camp, ostensibly so that the rest of the ghetto population could be saved. Such collaboration was later "rewarded" by the Nazis – sending Rumkowski and the remaining inmates to Auschwitz, where he perished.

The dehumanising of Auschwitz prisoners is described in Primo Levi's poem, *If This Is A Man*:

Consider if this is a man
Who works in the mud
Who does not know peace
Who fights for a scrap of bread
Who dies because of a yes or no.
Consider if this is a woman.
Without hair and without name
With no more strength to remember,
Her eyes empty and her womb cold
Like a frog in winter.

At times it seemed impossible to continue to believe in God. Elie Wiesel recounts an incident when a child had witnessed the hanging of another child "with the face of a sad angel". He heard someone groan:

"For God's sake, where is God?"
And from within me, I heard a voice answer:
"Where is he? This is where – hanging here from this gallows".

Yet many of these trampled-down people clung to their religious observances and traditions, celebrating Rosh Hashanah and Yom Yippur in the camps. Some even had the inner strength to sing the song of hope, the *Hatikvah,* as they were marched to the gas chambers.

There were, however, rare sparks of humanity and compassion shown by Germans to Jews. In August 1944, a Jewish pianist, Wladyslaw Szpilman, was hiding in an abandoned building in Warsaw where, fortuitously, there was a piano. He was discovered there by a German officer. To Szpilman's surprise, the officer did not arrest or kill him; after discovering that the emaciated Szpilman was a pianist, he asked him to play something.

Szpilman played Chopin's Nocturne in C-sharp minor. The officer told him that he was ashamed of being a German. He showed Szpilman a better place to hide and brought him bread and jam on numerous occasions. He also offered him one of his coats to keep him warm in the freezing temperatures. After the War, Szpilman discovered that his Samaritan was a Captain Wilm Hosenfeld, a devout Roman Catholic who had been a teacher and was vehemently opposed to National Socialism. Hosenfeld had been tortured by his Soviet captors, who thought that his claim to have saved a Jew was an outrageous lie. He died in a prisoner-of-war camp at Stalingrad, his spirit utterly broken.

A number of people put their lives at risk to provide Jews with safe passage to countries such as the UK and the USA. These included Frank Foley, Raoul Wallenberg, Nicholas Winton, and the American Unitarians Wainstill and Martha Sharp. Wainstill was a Unitarian minister who in 1933 occupied the pulpit of a small church in Meadville, Pennsylvania. He and his wife established an International Relations Club which discussed what to do for those 200,000 refugees from the Sudetenland who had crowded into Prague and needed immediate immigration to escape the Nazis. The Unitarian leadership in the USA started fund-raising and asked volunteers to carry the Unitarian witness to the Czech people. So, the Sharps set off to Prague in 1939. This was a huge personal sacrifice, as they had to leave their 7-year-old son and 2-year-old daughter behind in the USA.

Prague had a large Unitarian congregation, whose leader was Norbert Capek (see Chapter 10). Martha was particularly moved by the plight of the Jews in Prague: "I felt their dignity and their amazing capacity to rise above Nazi ill-treatment". The Sharps set themselves the daunting task of obtaining documentation for refugees to leave the country at a time when other countries – even the USA – were anti-immigrant and anti-Semitic. On numerous occasions, Martha accompanied refugees, many of them intellectuals, political leaders, and Jews, on perilous train journeys through Germany and then on to Holland, where they embarked on ships to England. Some of them were the orphans of parents who had decided to take their own lives rather than be tortured by the Nazis.

Eventually, however, Martha had to escape or be arrested by the Gestapo. So, the Sharps then transferred their lifeline to both Lisbon and Marseilles.

where they helped people escape from Vichy France as well as distributing milk to children. Between 1939 and 1940, they had helped as many as 3,500 refugees to escape from Nazi clutches.

On 9 September 2005, Martha and Waitstill Sharp were named by the historical remembrance organisation, Yad Vashem, as "Righteous Among the Nations". It is an honour given to Gentiles who risked their lives to help Jews escape the Holocaust despite danger to themselves and others. As Martha once said:

> *A series of miracles can happen when many people become concerned about an injustice and are willing to act together at the same time.*

Primo Levi warned us that we must understand where racial hatred springs from, and that we must be on our guard at all times to prevent it resurfacing. Yet these alarm bells were muffled as "ethnic cleansing" occurred in Rwanda, Bosnia, and Kosovo in the 1990s; when the Rohingya people were persecuted in 2015 and subsequent years; and in our current times as anti-Semitism once again raises its ugly head in Europe. There is no greater time than now for us to act together to defeat racism and make Martha Sharp's miracles happen.

Sources cited in this chapter

Primo Levi. If This Is A Man / The Truce. Abacus, 2013.

Martha and Waitstill Sharp. US Holocaust Memorial Museum. https://encyclopedia.ushmm.org/content/en/article/martha-and-waitstill-sharp

Wladyslaw Szpilman. The Pianist. Phoenix, 2000.

Elie Wiesel. Night. Penguin Books, 1985.

15 From Nothingness to Meaningfulness

No-one saves us but ourselves. No-one can and no-one may. We ourselves must walk the path...It is not the path to happiness. Happiness itself is the path.
(The Buddha)

Our greatest personal challenge is how to move from a meaningless life to a meaningful life across the abyss of nothingness. It is a path that is not dictated to us by an external spiritual authority; a path that is authentic to us as individuals. I suppose it is about searching for meaning in a universe that magnifies our insignificance. We are just one of a population of almost 8 billion in a world which is just one among more than 4.6 billion planets which is just one of 140 billion galaxies in the universe. It is almost too vast to comprehend, but if we think of a galaxy as being one frozen pea, then there would be enough of them to fill a Royal Albert Hall universe. In the words of the American cultural anthropologist, Ernest Becker:

Humans cannot endure their own littleness unless they can translate it into meaningfulness on the largest possible level.

Most of us are so overwhelmed by the enormity of the existentialist risk of human extinction that we don't spend much of our short time on earth pondering on it. After all, our descendants could potentially survive for a billion years before the expanding sun makes the earth uninhabitable. The apocalypse might, however, come much sooner. The Future of Humanity Institute at Oxford University warns that human extinction is more likely to result from anthropogenic causes than from natural causes. The greatest threats to the human species are man-made; artificial intelligence, global warming, nuclear war, and rogue biotechnology. The Doomsday Clock is a visual device, managed by the *Bulletin of Atomic Scientists,* to show how near we are to human extinction. Its minute hand stands at one hundred seconds to midnight. It is the responsibility of society today to push back the hand and reduce these existential risks.

With a few notable exceptions, such as Greta Thunberg, most of us dwell more on our own mortality than on the extinction of the human race. Perhaps at some time in your life you have found yourself isolated from the world, trapped in a bubble of nothingness. Once, when I was waiting for a train at Waterloo Station, I felt totally detached from the world as I saw everyone walking purposely to get home or to meet their lover on the platform. I felt rooted in some existentialist torpor unable physically to move forwards or backwards. This can even happen to a small child. The American physicist, Alan Lightman, recounts his experience.

> *My most vivid encounter with Nothingness occurred in a remarkable experience I had as a child of 9 years old. I was standing alone in a bedroom of my home in Memphis, Tennessee, gazing out the window at the empty street... I felt myself to be a tiny speck, insignificant in a vast universe that cared nothing about me or any living beings and their little dots of existence, a universe that simply was. And I felt that everything I had experienced in my young life, the joy and the sadness, and everything that I would later experience, meant absolutely nothing in the grand scheme of things.*

Lightman describes the experience as a realisation at once both liberating and terrifying. When the moment was over, he was back in his body. But for a fleeting moment he had experienced a profound absence of the familiar surroundings and thoughts that we create to anchor our lives. To him it was "a kind of Nothingness". As a small child, he had had a existentialist experience.

The philosophy of existentialism was founded in the early nineteenth century by the Danish theologian and philosopher Søren Kierkegaard. He acknowledged the despair and fear of mankind in the face of a God who is himself hidden; but he believed that this despair could be overcome by the awareness of divine grace. The philosopher Martin Heidegger saw existence as "that Being which is concerned in its being with its being". It lays bare the temporality of human existence and the fear of our own mortality. In achieving consciousness, we realise that the only certainty in life is that it will end – in either a bang or a whimper. We have been thrown into this world not of our making.

> *Has some Vast Imbecility*
> *Mighty to build and blend,*
> *But impotent to tend,*
> *Framed in jest, and left us now to hazardry?*
> *Nature's Questioning* by Thomas Hardy

But our existence does gives us the freedom to choose our own authentic life, but also the responsibility to avoid the pitfalls of choosing wrongly. In the words of the existentialist Jean-Paul Sartre, "Man is condemned to be free".

Our anxiety when faced with the absence of God-given rules for our ethical behaviour is captured in Edward Munch's painting, *The Scream*. The artist explained that he painted it after he "sensed an infinite scream passing through nature". It has been interpreted as depicting an existential crisis, a response to the distortion of the environment and of one's self.

In his essay *The Myth of Sisyphus*, Albert Camus uses the ancient Greek myth to depict a life inherently devoid of meaning and consequently absurd, which is the direct consequence of the absence of God. Sisyphus was a mortal who thought himself better than the gods. Zeus punished him by ordering him for all eternity to roll a boulder up a hill, only to watch it roll back down when he reached the top. Camus saw this as a perfect metaphor for the human condition:

> *Sisyphus teaches the higher fidelity that negates the gods and raises rocks. He too concludes that all is well. This universe henceforth without a master seems to him neither sterile nor futile. Each atom of that stone, each mineral flake of that night-filled mountain, in itself forms a world. The struggle itself toward the heights is enough to fill a man's heart. One must imagine Sisyphus happy.*

So, far from imprisoning us in existential angst, the lucid recognition of the absurdity of existence can liberate us from the belief in another life and permit us to live for the instant in the "implacable grandeur" of the "Now". The only thing more absurd about life's absurdity is to deny that absurdity and be trapped in a meaningless life.

But can a belief in God help us push our boulder up the hill and, more important, feel no angst as it rolls back? Can belief in God help overcome nothingness? A traditional view of God can offer consolation, particularly if we believe that we really won't die at all and will be rewarded for our good deeds in this life by admission into a blissful after-life. For us, free-thinking Unitarians, the answer is perhaps not that simple. The reward is not given externally and not outside our life on earth but perhaps can be earned authentically within ourselves. It is about developing a sense of self-empowerment, such as that described in the poem, *Invictus,* by the Victorian poet, William Ernest Henley. Nelson Mandela recited it to raise the spirits of his fellow prisoners on Robbin Island:

I thank whatever gods may be
For my unconquerable soul...

It matters not how strait the gate,
How charged with punishments the scroll,
I am the master of my fate,
I am the captain of my soul.

The novelist Anita Brookner has described the loneliness of the existentialist: "a saint without God; being your own hero, without all the sanction and support of religion or society".

In everyday life, most folk seem to come to terms with nothingness and put some meaning into their lives, even if they do not invoke God. But do they really? Just reflect on what the Buddhist, Stephen Batchelor says:

Everyone collaborates in everyone's forgetting nothingness. Parents seek to prepare their offspring for life. Social and political institutions are there to benefit the living. Religions offer consolation...We seek to arrange the details of our world in such a way that we feel secure, surrounded by what we like, protected against what we dislike.

His view is that once our material existence is more or less in order, we turn our attention to the psycho-management of our neuroses. But no matter how expertly we manage our lives, how convincing an image of well-being we project, we still find ourselves involved with what we hate and torn apart from what we love. We still don't get what we want and we still get what we don't want. True, we experience joy, success, love, bliss. But according to Batchelor, in the end we find ourselves once more prone to anguish:

> *We may know this, but do we understand it? We see it, are even overawed by it, but habit impels us to forget it. To cover it over and flee again to the lure of the tantalizing world. For were we to understand it, even in a glimpse, it might change everything.*

When asked about his teaching, Siddhartha Guatama, the Buddha (c. 490 BCE), stated that he taught about "anguish and the ending of anguish". He understood that anguish and suffering, *dukkha*, emanates from self-centred craving which dissipates into nothingness:

> *We all are running to reach the same goal, and that is Nothing! That is to say, whatever we do is futile if we look at its long-term consequence. When you know that your whole existence and even the existence of universe has to come an end at last, all your efforts and feverishness count as nothing. And your mind settles down to rest.*

The Buddha declares that he has found a central path by avoiding indulgence and mortification. He describes four ennobling truths; understanding anguish; letting go of its origins; realising its cessation; and cultivating the path leading to the cessation and to compassion.

It is said that the Buddha was kept immured within palaces by his father King Suddhodana, so as not to be distracted by the disquiet that reigned beyond its walls. But he became restless in his incarnation and longed to go out into the outside world. His father eventually relented, but tried to ensure that nothing distressing passed before his son's eyes. Despite these precautions, the Buddha chanced upon a person disfigured by disease, and another crippled by age, and a corpse, and a wandering monk. He was not only struck by the tragedy of anguish that he saw but thrown into questioning; questions to which he could not find a rational answer.

He became uneasy upon returning to the comforts of home. One night he stole away. For six years he drifted around the land, studying, meditating, subjecting himself to punishing ascetic rigours. With conventional options exhausted, he sat at the foot of a tree. Seven days later he awoke from the sleep of existential confusion. He now understood the nature of anguish. He let go of its origins. He brought into being a way of life.

What I admire about the Buddha is that he does not pretend to be a saviour of souls, but describes himself as a healer of the spirit. He believes that the root cause of anguish and suffering is self-centred craving. As Stephen Batchelor observes:

> *Anguish maintains its power and grip on our lives as long as we allow it to intimidate us. We must let go of craving before it crystallizes into anguish. Letting go of craving is not rejecting it but allowing it to be itself. Instead of forcibly freeing ourselves from it, we need to notice how its very nature is to free itself. Craving is nonsensical in a life which is in ceaseless mutation: emerging, modifying, disappearing. As soon as you grasp something, it is gone.*

As Bachelor states, no sooner than the cessation of craving is glimpsed, it is gone. It is like a momentary gap in the clouds. The sun shines brilliantly for a few moments, only to be covered over again. We find ourselves back in the humbling fog of anguish, craving, habit, restlessness, distraction. But with a difference: now we know where this track goes. We have set foot in the territory for which these words are just a map.

> *Although the road is never ending*
> *Take a step and keep walking,*
> *Do not look fearfully into the distance.*
> *On this path let the heart be your guide*
> *For the body is hesitant and full of fear.*
> Jalal ad-Din Muhammad Rumi

There is nothing particularly religious or spiritual about this path. It encompasses everything that we do. It is an authentic way of being in the world. It begins with how we understand the kind of reality that we inhabit, and the kind of thing we are that inhabit such a reality. We have a choice: either we can be our own jailers, by chaining ourselves to resentment of the past and fear of the future; or we can free ourselves by cutting the shackles of the self and surrendering to the well-being of existence as a whole. We need to scratch our name on ice and let the sun melt it away – for only the nameless can walk companionless on the path of selfless compassion.

Sources cited in this chapter

Stephen Batchelor. *Buddhism without Beliefs: A Contemporary Guide to Awakening.* Bloomsbury. 1997.

Albert Camus. *The Myth of Sisyphus and Other Essays.* Alfred A. Knopf, 1955.

Thich Nhat Hanh. *The Heart Of Buddha's Teaching: Transforming Suffering into Peace, Joy and Liberation: The Four Noble Truths, the Noble Eightfold Path, and Other Basic Buddhist Teachings.* Broadway Books, 1999.

Lightning Source UK Ltd.
Milton Keynes UK
UKHW012144130222
398631UK00003B/94

9 781838 169503